Meet the Teacher

How to Help Your Child
Navigate Elementary School

Meet the Teacher

How to Help Your Child Navigate Elementary School

A Common Sense Guide for Parents

Betty Borowski and Laura Mayne

FIREFLY BOOKS

A FIREFLY BOOK

Published by Firefly Books Ltd. 2010
Copyright © 2010 Firefly Books Ltd.
Text copyright © 2010 Betty Borowski and Laura Mayne
Illustrations copyright © Scot Ritchie

First printing

Library and Archives Canada Cataloguing in Publication
Borowski, Betty
Meet the teacher : how to help your child navigate elementary school /
Betty Borowski and Laura Mayne ; illustrator: Scot Ritchie. Includes index.
ISBN-13: 978-1-55407-660-4   ISBN-10: 1-55407-660-9
1. Education, Elementary--Parent participation.
2. Parent-teacher relationships. I. Mayne, Laura, 1957-
II. Title.
LB1048.5.B67 2010   372.119'2   C2010-903615-8

Publisher Cataloging-in-Publication Data (U.S.)
Borowski, Betty.
   Meet the teacher : how to help your child navigate elementary school /
Betty Borowski and Laura Mayne ; illustrated by Scot Ritchie.
[176] p. : ill. (some col.) ; cm. Includes index.
Chapters include: Entry Into School; Establishing a Positive Parent-Teacher Relationship;
Classroom and School Organization; Early Learning, Reading and Writing; Ways Children
Learn; Reading To and With Your Child; Math and Problem Solving; Study Skills and
Homework; Respect, Behavior and Discipline; Special Education; Report Cards and Parent-
Teacher Conferences; Conflict Resolution; Peer Pressure and Bullying; Parenting Strategies;
Try This at Home: Activity Ideas.
ISBN-13: 978-1-55407-660-4   ISBN-10: 1-55407-660-9
1. Parent-teacher relationships. 2. Education--Parent participation.
I. Mayne, Laura. II. Ritchie, Scot. III. Title.
371.1   dc22   LC225.B6769   2010

Published in the United States by
Firefly Books (U.S.) Inc.
P.O. Box 1338, Ellicott Station
Buffalo, New York 14205

Published in Canada by
Firefly Books Ltd.
66 Leek Crescent
Richmond Hill, Ontario L4B 1H1

Design and production: PageWave Graphics Inc.
Back cover photography credits:
Betty & Laura: Kristin Hohenadel; Scot: TJ Ngan

Printed in Canada

The publisher gratefully acknowledges the financial support for our publishing program by the Government of Canada through the Canada Book Fund as administered by the Department of Canadian Heritage.

Contents

Dedication

To quote Robert Munsch,
I'll love you forever,
I'll like you for always,
As long as I'm living
my baby you'll be.

To all my babies

To my biggest baby and strongest supporter, my husband Steve

To my first babies, my daughters Tessa and Kate

To my newest babies, my grandchildren,
Morgan, Julia and Amelia

bb

For Gerard and Maddy, my one particular harbour

lm

To Bill McNamara, our favorite principal ever

bb & lm

Introduction

A child's education is truly a team effort. Parents and teachers together are entrusted with the academic, social and emotional development of each child. This book is designed to provide parents with straightforward information and tips that will help make life easier for them and their children. Parents who have a clear understanding of how things work in the school and classroom are better able to focus on helping their child be happy and successful at school.

We discovered very early on during our 19 years of teaching at the same school that we both shared the same sense of humor and philosophy of teaching. For years, Betty's husband, Steve, would say, "You two should write a book." And here we are, recently retired from the classroom, but still very much interested and active in education, and wanting to share what we know.

Over the years, parents have asked us hundreds of questions about the ins and outs of school. We have addressed the questions parents asked us most often in these pages. You will find information on preparing your child for school, establishing a strong home-school link, homework, how to interpret a report card and how to handle different situations that may arise in your child's elementary school years.

We don't have any claim to fame. We just went to work every day, worked hard and had the time of our lives as teachers. After school, we went home, worked hard and had the time of our lives as moms and wives. At school and at home, we tried to do the same things: be organized, keep things simple, use humor and common sense.

We helped our own children navigate through elementary school with the benefit of understanding the system from the inside out. As teachers and moms, we offer you our accumulated knowledge in the hope that your child's journey through elementary school will be smooth sailing.

Chapter 1

Entry into School

The big day is finally here. You've been to the mall, the first-day-of-school outfit is all laid out, the brand new backpack has been packed, unpacked and repacked and your child's favorite snack is ready to go. Get the camera, charge that battery, it's the first day of school!

Whether your child is starting school for the first time or entering a new school, you want to prepare her, to ease any fears she may have, to have her greet that first day with excitement and a positive attitude in her carefully selected clothes and carrying that "just right" backpack.

Entering Kindergarten

Although many children attend daycare, nursery school or preschool programs, for most children, their first entry into the school system will be in kindergarten. In most school districts, kindergarten is offered, but it is optional. There is a great deal of variation in the set-up of kindergarten classes. There can be a half-day morning, half-day afternoon, full-day every other day or full-day every day.

Some programs have a staggered entry system where three to five students start school on the very first day, then another three to five more start the next day, and so on until all the students are present. If your school practices this system, make sure your child is aware of the exact day she will be starting school and how many more "sleeps" there will be until the big day. This is particularly important if there are older siblings starting on the first day of school and your kindergartener is not.

A child enters kindergarten based on his or her age. Each state or province has a cut-off date by which a child must have reached the age of entry in order to enroll in kindergarten. There can be exceptions to this rule for some special needs students, but exceptions are rare.

What can you do to help make sure your child is ready for kindergarten? Begin with the basics. Then consider the skills she should have, knowing that each child progresses at his or her own rate.

There are no academic requirements. However, if your child has a working knowledge or familiarity with the following list of skills, she will begin her school life with a great advantage. Most parents provide opportunities to learn and practice at least some of these skills as a part of everyday family life.

Basics
- Read to and with your child every day (see Chapter 6).
- Provide opportunities for your child to color, draw, print and write (see Chapter 5).
- Incorporate math learning into everyday family life (see Chapter 7).

Academic Skills
- Can count objects to 10
- Knows numbers from 1 to 10
- Knows colors
- Can name shapes (circle, triangle, square)
- Knows first and last name
- Recognizes first name on sight
- Independently prints first name. (There is a lot of unnamed work at school that cannot be handed back and young children do not always recognize their own work after the fact.)
- Recognizes and names letters of the alphabet (upper and lower case) and knows the sounds they make
- Can sort objects

Large Muscle Skills (Also Known as Gross Motor Skills)
- Stand (on one foot, on tiptoes)
- Run (skipping, galloping)
- Jump (both feet, take off on two feet and land on one foot, take off on one foot and land on one foot, take off on one foot and land on the other foot, jump forward, jump backwards)
- Hop (on both feet, on one foot)
- Kick a ball
- Roll and throw a ball
- Catch a ball
- Climb stairs

Small Muscle Skills (Also Known as Fine Motor Skills)
- Can draw (shapes, person)
- Applies glue in as neat a fashion as possible
- Cuts using scissors properly
- Colors using crayons, colored pencils or markers
- Holds a book correctly and turn pages carefully
- Can print (first name)
- Can hold a pencil properly (see illustration on on the next page)

How to Hold a Pencil

The proper grip is the tripod grip using the thumb and first two fingers. A way to teach this grip is to take a small piece of paper crumpled up into a ball about the size of a grape and have the child practice picking it up and dropping it repeatedly, using the thumb and first two fingers. After a bit of practice, have the child pick up a pencil just above the sharpened end using the same grip. Help her rest the pencil on her hand and grip the pencil firmly, but not tightly, with fingers slightly bent.

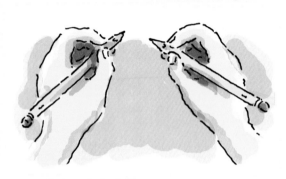

Social Skills

- Uses good manners (please, thank you, you're welcome, excuse me, I'm sorry)
- Covers mouth when yawning and yawns quietly
- Coughs or sneezes into elbow rather than hand. (Many teachers call this "the Dracula" as raising your elbow to your mouth looks like Dracula holding up his cape across his mouth.)
- Uses a napkin
- Able to sit still and listen to a story

Self-help and Self-care Skills

- Is able to use washroom independently
- Washes and dries hands. (Hand washing should last as long as it takes to sing "Happy Birthday.")
- Is able to dress and undress self (outer clothing, including fasteners and zippers)
- Can put on own shoes and boots
- Can open, close and pack own backpack

Preparing for the First Day of School

Registration Documentation

Most schools have kindergarten registration times set up as early as February for the following school year. Call the school for specific details. Be prepared when you register your child, as you must present some or all of the following documents:

- birth certificate or passport of child
- proof of residence (usually a utility bill)
- child's immunization record (most states also require proof of tuberculosis skin test)
- proof of citizenship or landed immigrant status
- child's health card (in Canada)
- emergency contact information

If your child has any special needs, severe allergies or other medical conditions, be sure you inform the school and fill out the necessary paperwork when you register. Check back between registration day and the first day of school to be sure that all necessary arrangements are in place and the teacher has been notified.

Visit the School

To help your child make the transition from home to school or from preschool to "big school," visit the school and do a walkabout. Check in at the school office first. You might have an opportunity to do this when you register your child. Many schools offer a visit and short orientation before the first day of school. Your child may already be familiar with the school if she has older siblings.

Transportation

Where you live in relation to the school will dictate how your child gets to school. Each school district has its own policy on bus eligibility. You will be given information on this at registration. Children who do not take the bus either walk, ride a bike or are driven to school. Each school has its own drop-off area and entry routines. Most schools have a designated kindergarten yard.

Practice Runs

Do some practice runs with your child that include getting up, having breakfast, getting dressed, washed, hair combed or brushed, packing the knapsack (best done the night before), and getting out the door and to school on time. This can be challenging if you have more than one child, so it is best to know what time to set the alarm clock. It is very important for your child to be on time for school. If your child takes the bus, you need to know what time the bus arrives at your stop. Bus drivers have a tight schedule and cannot wait for stragglers.

Walking Bus

A "walking bus" is a group of kids that walks to school under the supervision of an adult. Children wait at a designated stop and are picked up along the route. This system is organized by parent volunteers in the neighborhood and not by the school. The advantages of a walking bus are that kids get fresh air and exercise, children are safe, supervision can be shared by many parents on a rotating basis and it is a green initiative that reduces your carbon footprint.

Talk It Up

Talk to your child about what school will be like. Tell her that school will be fun, she will make new friends, the teacher will read wonderful stories to her, she'll play and sing, and all the time she will be learning.

Remind her that you expect her to listen to the teacher, obey the rules and work hard. Every day, encourage your child to talk about what happened at school. Ask her what activities did she do, what are the names of her friends, what stories did they read and what songs did they sing. It's all in the questioning. Ask if anyone visited the classroom, if the class went to the library or the gym and what happened there. Did they go outside and were there any surprises?

Goodbye Routine

Some children run into the schoolyard on the first day of kindergarten without so much as a backward glance while others are glued to the sides of their parents. Whichever category your child falls into, she will feel more confident entering the classroom on the first day and every day with the help of a goodbye routine which you and your child can create and practice together before the first day of school. Develop a special hug, saying or other short ritual together.

Practice your routine many times before school starts, such as when you drop your child off for a play date, lesson or at Grandma's house. The comfort of a routine will help your child separate from you more easily. Rather than focusing on the goodbye, leave your child with a reminder of things you plan to do when you are together again. If your child has extreme separation anxiety, speak with the teacher for further tips. Be sure your child knows who will pick her up and what will happen when the school day ends.

Good Habits

It is important to have a good bedtime and morning routine in place. A five-year-old child needs 10 to 12 hours of sleep each night. Give yourself enough time in the morning so your family is not in panic mode trying to get out the door on time. Build in time for a healthy breakfast and for good daily hygiene, which includes freshly brushed hair and teeth. Bathing regularly is a must, as are neat and clean clothes. Be sure your child is dressed appropriately for the day's activities (for example, gym day) and for the weather.

Equipping Your Child for School

Dress your child in clothing, shoes and boots that can be put on and taken off independently. If your child cannot tie his own shoelaces, buy slip-on shoes or ones with Velcro fasteners. For safety reasons, many schools ask parents to provide a pair of shoes that will stay at school. These are called "indoor shoes" and are worn in place of wet, muddy or snowy outdoor boots or shoes. Make every effort to teach your child how to zip up his own jacket. Picture this: a lone kindergarten teacher in a room of 20 or more children, none of whom can do up a zipper, put on their own boots, do up their own backpack or get the backpack onto their back. And you think you have trouble getting out the door on time! Most children just need a little practice with zippers and boots and they will be independent in no time.

Some schools ask for a set of clothing, including underwear, to be sent in from home and clearly labeled with the child's name. These are kept at school in case of an emergency (a washroom, mud or paint mishap).

A school bag or backpack should be big enough to hold a snack, shoes, library book (Murphy's law says that your child will sign out the largest book in the library), newsletter, schoolwork (including giant paintings), etc. Have your child practice carrying, packing, unpacking and zipping up the bag until he can do this on his own.

Kindergarten FAQs

Is there a special kindergarten yard? Is there supervision in this yard before the bell rings? Is there a recess? Where should I drop off and pick up my child?
Answers to these questions will vary depending on the school. Many schools offer an interview or orientation before the first day of school to provide all the necessary information and answer any questions parents may have. If an orientation is not offered, contact the school with your questions.

What if somebody different is picking my child up from school?
Tell the teacher ahead of time and give the name of the person who will be picking up your child or call the school office and leave a message to be relayed to the teacher.

Is there a washroom in the kindergarten classroom?
Most Kindergarten classrooms have their own washroom. If not, there is one close by.

Will the teacher assist my child in the washroom?
Unless your child has special needs, the answer is no.

Does the teacher administer medication?
The teacher does not give medication to children. In certain cases, school personnel may administer prescription medications, but this procedure varies in different school districts.

What if my child has a peanut allergy?
If your child has a peanut allergy, you should notify the school and talk with the classroom teacher well in advance of the first day of school. There are specific forms to be filled out, EpiPens to be stored and procedures to be followed to ensure your child's safety. Your child should already be aware that she has an allergy and know that she must eat only foods brought from home. Check with the school regarding a "Peanut Free Program." Most school staffs have been fully trained in the use of EpiPens. See Chapter 3 on School and Classroom Organization and Procedures.

What do I do if my child's classmate has a severe food allergy?

You will be notified by the classroom teacher if there are any children in the class with severe food allergies and instructed as to what foods are allowed and not allowed.

When should I keep my child home from school?

If he has a fever, very runny nose and or a bad cough, severe sore throat or earache, diarrhea, vomiting, head lice or any contagious disease he should be kept home. If in doubt, check with a doctor.

Won't my child's belongings get mixed up with somebody else's?

Label all your child's personal items with her name.

Should I send a snack to school with my child? If so, what should I send?

Most kindergarten programs allow time for a snack. Schools usually ask that the snack be nutritious. Avoid sending nut products. It is very helpful if your child can open the snack container independently and eat the snack in the short amount of time provided. We have witnessed kindergarten students who have a veritable buffet of four or five items for snack each day. One tiny little girl had a huge submarine sandwich so tightly wrapped in plastic wrap that she was still unwrapping the sandwich when the rest of the students had finished eating, playing and were getting ready to go home.

Some healthy and easy to eat snacks are:

- muffins
- fruit or raw vegetables that are washed, cut up and ready to eat
- pretzels
- cheese and crackers
- small yogurt (plus spoon)
- pudding, fruit or jello cup (plus spoon)
- goldfish crackers
- half a sandwich
- water, juice or milk* (not soda pop)
  *Many schools ask that drinks be in reusable containers.

First Day of School Each Year

It is normal for children to feel simultaneously excited and scared about the first day of school each year. As with children preparing for kindergarten, it is important for children of any age to be as ready as they can be for the first day. In the weeks before school begins, you should:

Talk with your child about the upcoming year, get her to share how she is feeling and ask if she has any concerns. Also talk about anything that will be different this year, such as having a new teacher, being in school all day, playing in a different part of the playground (some schools divide the students by grade levels) or staying at school for lunch instead of coming home each day. Once you receive the curriculum outline for your child's new grade, use it as a springboard for discussion with your child about upcoming topics of study and what to look forward to in the new school year.

If she rides the bus, check with the school to **see if there are any changes in the bus schedule.**

Stock up on supplies. In the last weeks before school begins some schools send out a list of required supplies. Take your child with you when you shop so she can pick out her own supplies. Even if there isn't a list of required items, your child will enjoy picking out some cool new pencils or a new pack of markers. Betty's husband, Steve, has an excellent theory: if spending a few bucks on new colored pencils, notebooks and other school supplies is going to make your child feel happy and excited about returning to school, then your money is well spent.

Let your child pick out her own outfit for the first day. It doesn't have to be brand new, but it should be something she feels confident and comfortable in.

Even if the family budget does not allow for the purchase of a new backpack, clothing or supplies, **try to manage a small treat** to make your child feel excited about returning to school (a new hair accessory or a new T-shirt for the first day).

Keep your child's mind active during the summer holidays by continuing to read, visiting the library, signing up for summer programs, doing family activities that encourage learning (playing board games, cards, writing in a journal, making a scrapbook of summer activities and excursions).

School Avoidance

Sometimes it happens that a perfectly healthy child starts coming down with school-day tummy aches, headaches or other symptoms that are conspicuously absent on days when there is no school.

Acknowledge your child's symptoms and make an appointment to see the doctor. If no physical cause is found, talk to your child to see if there is something bothering her at school. It could be that your child is feeling separation anxiety, is having problems with other children at school, is struggling with schoolwork, has a fear of the teacher or is experiencing either the threat of bullying or actual bullying. Share this information with your child's teacher. Try to get to the bottom of the problem, but you may discover that you can't pinpoint the cause of the problem. If the doctor determines there is nothing physically wrong with your child and gives the okay for her to return to school, be gentle but firm. Let your child know that the expectation is that she has to go to school. Assure her that you will work things through together. If she has been away from school for a few days, you may want to start with only a half day and ease her back to full-day attendance to reduce her anxiety level about returning.

If the problem persists or escalates, make another appointment with the doctor.

Reestablish good bedtime and morning habits. This may be somewhat difficult after a summer of more relaxed living, but it is important. There are two schools of thought about this subject. One is to readjust bedtime and wakeup time by 15 minutes every few days until the regular school-day times are reached. The second is just to get back into the routine cold turkey on the first day of school and be prepared for a few days of tiredness. However, most experts agree that children five to nine years old should get 10 or more hours of sleep, children nine to 12 years old should get nine or 10 hours of sleep and teenagers should get eight to 10 hours of sleep.

Remind your child that each new school year is a fresh start and a clean slate. If the previous school year was not a positive experience for your child, she will be pleased to be starting over. If it was a happy and successful year, remind her to continue doing the things that made it that way: working hard, listening well and co-operating with her teacher and classmates.

Changing Schools

There are a number of reasons why a student might change schools:
- Transitioning from one level of education to the next (elementary school to middle school to high school)
- Moving to a new home
- Attending a specialty program (second language, gifted, special needs)
- Switching from one type of school to another (public to private)
- Deciding to move a child to a new school because of on-going problems
- Seeking a school with a different philosophy
- Relocating to another school because of expulsion

When changing schools, the process is similar to the one you followed when you initially registered your child for kindergarten. Again, you must bring in registration documentation. See page 13. When transferring to another school within the same state or province, your child's school records will automatically be sent on to the new school. When entering a school in a different state, province or country, records are not transferred. It is up to you to pass on a copy of your child's most recent report cards, sample work and any other pertinent documentation to the new school. Grade placement is generally based on chronological age unless there are mitigating factors. Some schools may require students to write a grade placement test or show your child's results of standardized testing.

Don't hold back any academic, personal or social information as teachers cannot program effectively if these details are missing. Parents sometimes believe they are giving their child a fresh start by holding back vital information. Here is an example. A child with an identified, serious behavior problem was transferred into our school. The parents did not divulge the family doctor's diagnosis to the school, thinking that perhaps things would be different this time around. In the meantime, the child was violent, did not get off to a "good" start, caused minor injuries to the teacher and fellow students and a lot of time was wasted trying to piece together what was going on.

Tips to Ease the Transition
- Listen to your child's feelings and concerns about the change.
- Acknowledge your child's feelings and let her know that it's okay

to feel happy, sad, apprehensive, nervous and excited, sometimes all at the same time.
- Give your child extra support and keep checking in to see how she is doing.
- Try to match programs from the old school to the new school. (If the child takes and enjoys instrumental music, try to find a school that offers it.)
- Talk a lot about the old school and make sure your child has a proper goodbye.
- Keep in touch with friends from the old school.
- Talk a lot about the new school and accentuate the positive.

How to Say Goodbye to Classmates
- Help your child make a gift for a special friend.
- Have a little party for your child's friends before you move.
- Have your child make a scrapbook with pictures and mementos from the old school.
- Have your child's classmates sign a class photo.
- Arrange ways of staying in touch with special friends.

Tips for Making Friends
It can be difficult to be "the new kid on the block." Some children make friends easily and sail through transitions, whereas others are shy and find it difficult to approach people they don't know. You know your child and will be able to tailor these tips to his personality.

Young children should:
- Talk to the teacher (or you can talk to the teacher) about arranging a "show and tell" session for your child. With your child, select some photos and other items he can to bring to class as an introduction to who he is and where he came from
- Smile and be themselves
- Join in games and playground activities
- Start a conversation by complimenting someone on their shirt, shoes or backpack
- Ask other children questions about themselves
- Invite a new friend over to play
- Be kind to the next new kid who comes to the class

Tweens should:
- Hang out with kids they would like to be friends with
- Smile and be themselves
- Start a conversation about something neutral like a TV show or music
- Make an effort to join an extracurricular activity they enjoy
- Strike a balance between talking and listening to others
- Not brag or sound selfish
- Invite a new friend home
- Be considerate of the next new kid

Newcomers to the Country/ English Language Learners

People who are new to a country face unique challenges. There can be cultural differences, language differences and an overwhelming number of new things to learn.

Starting a new school without knowing the language can be very difficult. Some school districts have a reception center where families new to the country are welcomed and receive assistance with school registration. These reception centers also offer links to settlement support agencies in the community. The services offered include help in finding housing, employment and English language classes.

At the reception center, children will be assessed to determine their level of English language proficiency. This information is passed on to the school that the child will be attending and school staff are alerted to the child's needs at the time of registration. School districts that do not have a reception center have trained staff members who conduct an assessment of a child's school level. Children are generally placed in an age-appropriate classroom. If a child has had limited schooling in his home country, assistance will be given to help him make up what he has missed.

Instruction in English is provided to students by the classroom teacher and a qualified English Language Learner (ELL) teacher. The ELL teacher may work in the classroom with the child or withdraw the child from the classroom for part of the day. Grade level expectations for ELL students are modified according to the student's knowledge of English. Students are then evaluated according to the modified expectations. Parents are encouraged to take a friend or relative along to parent-teacher conferences as a translator, if necessary. Some school districts offer translation services.

In the classroom, ELL students are welcomed, given a tour of the school, taught basic survival language (such as the location of washrooms) and teamed up with a group of buddies who will help them settle in and feel comfortable in the classroom.

Cultural differences in a new country can also be confusing. For example, in some countries shaking your head from side to side means "yes," while in North America, that head motion would mean "no." In many countries, children stand up when answering a question in class. Here, classrooms are less formal and children are allowed to remain seated when answering a question. It takes time to learn all the customs of a new country and children are given instruction on these customs and routines as part of their English instruction.

It takes approximately two years for a child to speak English with fluency, and five to seven years to achieve academic proficiency. Children who are fluent readers and writers in their first language have an easier time learning to speak, read and write in English. Children should be read to both in their first language and in English. ELL students are encouraged to write in their first language as well. At home, parents should try to strike a balance between speaking their first language and speaking English. Many children learn English at a faster rate than their parents as they are immersed in it each day at school.

Tips for Parents of ELL Students

- If children are reluctant about starting school in a new language, remind them of other things they have done that were difficult at first but became easier after they tried doing them.
- Encourage children to make friends in the new school and invite a new friend to your home.
- Let your children see you making friends and becoming integrated into the community. This will help them to take those same steps more confidently.
- Encourage your children to participate in classroom and school activities.
- Get your child involved in an extracurricular activity such as a sports team, a club or lessons. Ask teachers at school or the librarian at your public library about extracurricular activities that are available in your area. The library is also a great source for community information.

There are many things you can do to help your child be successful when entering school, either for the first time or a new grade.

When preparing a child for kindergarten:
- Work with her on basic academic, social, motor and self-help skills
- Be informed about school and classroom procedures
- Complete all registration requirements
- Visit the school
- Do some practice runs
- Establish routines (goodbye, bedtime, morning)
- Talk with your child about what to expect

When preparing your child for a new grade:
- Talk about what to expect
- Keep your child's mind active during the summer
- Be sure your child has the required supplies
- Reestablish bedtime and morning routines
- Familiarize yourself with the curriculum so your child knows what to look forward to

When changing schools:
- Complete moving procedures and registration requirements
- Share all pertinent information with the new school
- Help make your child's transition as smooth as possible

Chapter 2

Establishing a Positive Relationship with Your Child's Teacher

You will always be the first and most important teacher in your child's life. Your home is the first school in your child's life. When he enters the elementary school system and begins to spend up to six hours a day at school, his classroom teacher also becomes a huge influence. Ideally, responsibility for the child's education is shared between you and the teacher, as you both have distinct roles to play. A positive working relationship with your child's teacher is crucial to the progress, development and happiness of your son or daughter.

In our combined 57 years of teaching, we have met and worked with well over 1,000 families. Almost every one of the parent-teacher relationships we have formed has been cordial, positive, productive, rewarding and, in some cases, lasting. We have had the pleasure of getting to know whole families very well through teaching or meeting all the siblings. How delightful it has been over the years to receive from parents or students tokens of appreciation, such as a coffee in the morning, a bag of craft materials for the class, gifts for the births of our own children, letters of support and thanks, and foil-wrapped bouquets of flowers from the garden. We have loved sharing with parents stories of funny things their child has said or done, important moments such as the day "the light went on" and outstanding achievements. These parent-teacher relationships work because they operate on a give-and-take basis. They are founded on mutual respect, open and honest communication, and a genuine, shared sense of pride in the accomplishments of the child.

Don't Be Afraid to Talk to Your Child's Teacher

Some parents are intimidated by, or feel timid around, the teacher. Teachers are not as scary as you might think. Teachers are people too. They have families to care for, mortgages to pay, doctor's appointments to keep, homes to clean, dinners to make. Sound familiar? As well as these everyday realities of life, you and the teacher have something else in common, and that is an interest in your child. If you are anxious and feel as though you have been transported back in time to your own school days when the teacher was a larger-than-life authority figure, remember that you are now an adult and on equal footing with the teacher. Go ahead and speak up.

There are parents who hesitate to contact or question the teacher when an issue arises. They are afraid of making the teacher angry and worried that the teacher will "take it out" on their child. In this situation, it is best to be honest and say, "I am worried that if I tell you this it will make things worse for my child. Can we please talk about it?" This is a very difficult thing for some parents to do, but you have every right to do it. Be prepared and be polite. In most cases things are sorted out and there are no repercussions for your child. If things do not go smoothly, see Chapter 12: Conflict Resolution.

Understanding the Teacher's Limitations

Some parents want the teacher's full attention focused on their child and only their child. The teacher cannot devote 100 percent of their attention to only one child. By necessity, a classroom of many children has to be run differently than the family unit. Every student in the class is someone's precious child and the teacher must balance the needs of all of them. Home is the place where your child shines as brightly as a star. At school, he is one of many in a string of lights.

Hovering parents over-involve themselves in their child's school life and are constantly calling the teacher or showing up unannounced to question, complain or comment on marks, routines, lessons, policies and minor incidents. These parents have too much contact with their child's teacher, are trying to micromanage everything and often bail out their child. "How come my child got such a small slice of pizza for lunch on pizza day?" "I don't like the mark my child received." "My child is not forming the letter 'f' correctly in handwriting." "You didn't give my child enough time to eat his lunch." "My child didn't know there was a test today." This type of parent creates a reputation for being difficult.

Resolving Your Concerns with a Teacher

There are a small number of parents who consider the teacher "the enemy." They misconstrue the teacher's handling of a situation as dislike of their child. They make the assumption that wrong has been done to their child. They often jump to conclusions before checking out what has actually happened. In this situation, it is the child who suffers. He feels tension, may be embarrassed by the parent's behavior, witnesses poor role modeling and does not receive the unified support of parent and teacher. If there is a legitimate concern, it should, of course, be addressed. Being calm and using positive ways to express concerns will almost certainly result in a smoother conversation and a resolution.

If there is a difference of opinion between you and the teacher, it is in everyone's best interest to keep negative comments from reaching your child's ears. Children love their parents and are usually very attached to their teachers and a parent-teacher conflict puts the child in the middle. Young children may feel awkward and confused, and older children may feel that your criticism of the teacher gives them free rein to disrespect and badmouth the teacher. Keep in mind that your child will most likely copy the problem-solving strategies that you use.

How to Address Concerns Effectively

- Introduce yourself, make eye contact, shake hands, smile.
- Speak in a polite, calm and even tone.
- Be assertive, but not aggressive.
- Be sure your body language and gestures are not threatening (no finger wagging).
- Be well informed.
- Differentiate between important concerns and those that are trivial.
- Know what you want to communicate.
- Strike a balance between speaking and listening.
- Try to be open and accepting of what you hear.
- Keep things in perspective.

Forming a Positive Relationship with the Teacher

Teachers have valuable insights into how your child functions in a classroom setting, his learning style and behavior, just as you have valuable insights from the home perspective. Feel free to enlighten the teacher with the observations you have made about your child. Never hesitate to ask questions about your child's development and progress at school.

When you and the teacher work together as a team, share information and responsibility, the whole child is best served. The teacher may see things about your child, for better or worse, that you don't see, so try to accept these comments in the manner in which they are offered. As our favorite principal used to say, "We don't make this stuff up, we just report it."

Most teachers have chosen their career based on the fact that they like kids and love to impart knowledge and help children learn, not, as is commonly thought, to have a long summer holiday and two weeks off at Christmas. All teachers have a post-secondary degree (or two) that includes extensive training in the following areas: curriculum, assessment and evaluation, instructional methods, classroom management, multiculturalism and diversity and many others. Teachers also take evening, weekend and summer courses to upgrade their skills, and read professional books and journals to stay current. Here are some ways to develop a good working relationship with your child's teacher.

Familiarize Yourself with How the School and Classroom are Run

- Most schools have a website that contains basic information such as the school hours, phone number, calendar of events (holidays, early dismissal days, no school days) staff list, lunch and recess times, bus information, student absence routine and school policies.
- The first newsletter from the school will contain a lot of the above information. It's a good idea to have a special place in your home for any correspondence from school so that you can locate it quickly. Many families post a calendar on the fridge and write important school dates on it. This is particularly helpful if you have more than one child.
- Go to the school, walk around, go inside, introduce yourselves to the principal, secretary, custodian and teacher (if possible), to get a feel for the environment.
- Sign and return, on time, your child's agenda or daily planner, tests and assignments, permission/trip/lunch forms, report cards and information forms.
- Note routines and help your child be organized by making sure he packs the correct materials for the day—lunch, library book, gym clothes, uniform for extracurricular sports, special clothing for an excursion, props for a classroom play, etc.
- Know the name of your child's teacher and what grade he is in. Here's a scenario we've seen many times. A parent comes into

the office carrying a lunch and the secretary asks, "Who is your child's teacher?" The dad says (sorry, dads, but it is usually the father), "Um, I don't know." It's not a bad idea to know as many staff members as possible. This will help you to become part of the school community, and your child will likely be taught by one of these teachers in future years.

- Whenever possible, attend school functions such as concerts, movie nights and curriculum nights.
- Volunteer your services, if you are able, in the classroom. For example, be a guest speaker or a class trip supervisor.

Make Contact with the Teacher Early in the School Year

Most schools have an open house or curriculum night in the first month or so. Make every effort to attend this event just to introduce yourself to this year's teacher and get a feel for the physical setting of the school. Your child will want to show you off and have you meet their teacher and to see their classroom. This is an informal, first-time meeting and definitely not an interview. Any specific questions or concerns about your child should be addressed at a separate meeting, as the teacher will be busy meeting and greeting all the parents.

- If your work hours do not allow you to attend school events, you can introduce yourself by phone or through a note.
- As early in the year as possible, share with the teacher any pertinent information about your child.

If your family faces financial hardships, speaking to a school administrator will offer you privacy and save you from having to share this information with each teacher, if you have more than one

---

Things to Share with the Teacher

- Medical conditions
- Family circumstances (custody issues, changes such as a new baby or serious illness in the family)
- Information about glasses, retainers, etc.
- Learning issues
- Techniques that work with your child
- Feel free to share anything fun or exciting or anything that can help the teacher get to know your child better.

child. There is often special funding available for school trips, special lunch days, etc.

Ways to Contact the Teacher

- Send a note to the teacher with your child.
- Make a note in the student's agenda or homework book.
- Call the school and leave a message for the teacher. Keep in mind that during recess and lunch breaks teachers may have supervision duty, may be in the bathroom or may be sitting down for the first quiet moment of their day having a cup of coffee. Therefore, your call may not be returned immediately.
- Call the school to set up a meeting. If you cannot keep your appointment, call the school to cancel and reschedule.
- E-mail the teacher (varies within different school districts). If your school does not allow you to contact teachers by e-mail, it is likely a teacher union issue or school board policy and is out of the teacher's hands.

Things that Are Not a Good Idea

- Calling a teacher at home
- Showing up at the classroom door expecting an immediate meeting
- Speaking in the heat of anger
- Expecting an instant resolution or response
- Trying to e-mail the teacher if it is not school policy
- Criticizing the teacher in front of the child
- Bailing your child out and never letting him suffer the consequences of his actions

Address Issues as They Arise

If there's something you are concerned about, don't feel you have to wait until the official interview time to discuss it with the teacher. Your question may well have a simple answer and the issue could be readily resolved. If it's a more complicated situation, it's always best to get a jumpstart on it. A phone call, sometimes followed by an in-person sharing of information, may be necessary.

Chain of Command

The classroom teacher should always be your first point of contact. If you have met with the teacher and the issue is unresolved, you can then contact the school principal or vice principal, who will arrange to meet with you and the teacher. If the problem has still not been resolved, you may wish to contact the supervisory officer. Very few issues should escalate to that level. Most teachers and principals are capable and willing to solve problems as they arise. They have years of training and experience in these matters. After a resolution has been reached and some time has passed, be sure to follow up with the teacher as well as your child to see how things are going.

Don't jump the gun and go immediately to the highest level. You will, most likely, be directed back to your school administrators. Sometimes if people don't get the answer they want to hear, they escalate an issue in the hope of a more favorable response. But you should give serious thought and consideration to what the professionals are telling you, and remember that everyone is working in the best interests of your child.

Treat the parent-teacher relationship as you would any other professional relationship, like that between you and your family doctor, for instance.

- Learn school and classroom procedures and events
- Keep the lines of communication open
- Make contact early in the school year
- Address issues as they arise
- Address issues in a positive and constructive way
- Make an appointment, show up on time, call if you will be late or need to cancel
- Always deal with the teacher first
- Know that you and the teacher are working for a common purpose

Chapter 3

School and Classroom Organization and Procedures

Kindergarten kids think the custodian is "the boss" of the school. Smart parents, teachers and principals know that the secretary has her finger on the pulse of all that goes on in the school. In actual fact, it takes the custodian, the school secretary, the principal, the teachers, the kids and smart parents to make a great school.

For some parents the decision on where to send their child to school is as easy as "Where's the closest school?" For others, the decision is overwhelming and presents a daunting task as they try to find that "great" school.

There are many kinds of schools. It is compulsory in the United States and Canada for children to attend school, but the age range for entry into school varies by state and province. Choosing a school could involve some homework on your part to determine the best fit for your family.

The School Team

Once you have chosen a school for your child, you should familiarize yourself with the many staff members who make up the school team.

School Staff
- principal (also called an administrator)
- vice-principal (also called an administrator)
- secretary
- classroom teachers
- specialty teachers such as a librarian, special education teacher, teaching English to speakers of other languages (TESOL) teacher (also called ESL or ELL), music teacher, physical education teacher, art teacher, planning time teacher
- caretaker (also called custodian)
- pre-service teachers (also called student teachers) studying to be teachers. Pre-service teachers spend periods of time in classrooms and work with certified teachers to gain experience
- substitute teachers (also called supply teachers) take over a class when the regular teacher is absent.
- support workers, also called teaching assistants, paraprofessionals, ERWs (Educational Resource Workers), work with special needs children to assist the child with any physical or academic needs
- long-term occasional (LTO) teacher fills in for teachers on leave

• support staff such as school psychologist, speech and language pathologist, social worker, child and youth worker, consultants for various needs will come into the school when required

Allotment and Assignment of Teachers

It is the school administrator, usually called the principal, who makes staffing decisions. He or she is usually allotted a certain number of teachers by the school district based on the number of students in the school. The principal calculates the number of classes in the school based on the teacher-pupil ratio, which varies from state to state and from province to province. The principal then assigns a teacher to a specific grade and class. Teachers are often given the opportunity to provide input on which grade they would like to teach, but the final decision rests with the principal. The teacher's qualifications and the number of years they have already taught in the grade are taken into account when placements are made.

Depending on the number of children in the school and the number of teachers allotted to the school, there may be a combination of single grades and combined grades in the school. The typical classroom setup includes straight grade, combined (or split) grade or multi-age classes, rotary classes (in which the kids rotate or the teachers rotate), team teaching or job sharing.

Teachers

Every teacher brings his or her own teaching style, areas of expertise, personality, strengths and weaknesses to the job. In the school we taught at for many years, one teacher had the gift of raising each child's self esteem, one teacher brought the arts to life with her students and another ran his classroom firmly, fairly and with a great sense of humor.

If your child has a new-to-the-profession teacher, how lucky for him. Rookie teachers bring energy, freshness and the latest in teaching philosophies, methodologies and ideas to their classroom. Their first class will always be near and dear to their heart. New teachers are usually under the wing of a mentor who oversees, advises and guides them. Workshops, meetings and other supports for new teachers are offered by the school district.

Seasoned teachers bring years of experience working with children and their parents to the classroom, as well as tried and true techniques. They have an ease and confidence that comes from years of familiarity with children and the system, and a vast accumulation of knowledge and experience.

As in every profession, there is a range of competency. There are amazing teachers, excellent teachers, wonderful teachers, great teachers, good teachers, adequate teachers and, sadly, there are poor teachers. There is a difference between a poor teacher and a "bad" teacher. A poor teacher may be disorganized, take a long time to mark and return work, lack strong class management skills or have a lackluster method of delivering the program. A truly incompetent teacher has ongoing problems in many areas: cannot manage student behavior, cannot deliver the program effectively, does not know the content and may have attitudes that can be damaging to the child's academic progress and emotional health. See Chapter 12 for more information on how to deal with teachers who are struggling or incompetent.

Classroom Placement

The process of making up classes for the start of the school year usually begins in the spring. The principal receives information about the number of teachers allocated to the school based on projected enrollment. In most places, once the principal has assigned a teacher to each grade and class, a team consisting of administrators, the current classroom teacher, the receiving classroom teacher and support staff meets. The purpose of the meeting is to assign a student to a class with a teacher who will best suit their learning style and educational needs, and will offer the best chance of student success.

The following factors are taken into consideration when making up classes:

- the academic and social needs of the child
- the child's learning style
- boy–girl ratio in the class
- the balance of ability levels of all students in the class
- the social dynamics within the class
- the best placement of special needs students
- whether the student is best suited to a straight grade or combined class
- needs of twins or multiples

Sometimes, the school's organization plans that were carefully laid out in the spring need to be altered in the fall due to changes in enrollment. This could mean the school gains or loses teachers, resulting in the reorganization of classes, even after the school year has begun. Although this is not the best scenario for teachers or students, adjustments are usually made fairly quickly.

Combined Grades

Some parents are concerned when their child is placed in a combined (split) grade classroom. In any classroom, straight or combined, there is a large range of abilities among the students. The teachers in any classroom are trained to work with students at their own level. Each grade in a combined class follows a separate curriculum specific to that grade. If the whole class is studying one topic, the expectations will vary by grade.

Parent Request for Student Placement

Parents often wish to have input into the class placement of their child. In our experience, most parent requests fall into two categories: "I want my child to be in the same class as his friend," and "I want my child to be in a specific teacher's class." Having friends and social interaction at school is very important for children, but it is not a sound reason for class placement. Friends can mingle before school, at recess, at lunch and after school.

Be aware that by making a request, you may be undoing a placement that was carefully thought out by school staff. The professional judgment of the school team qualifies them to make the best placement for every child in the school, as they can see "the big picture." Trust in their ability to make a good decision.

Some schools invite parent requests, but ask that you refer only to your child, not mentioning other students by name and that you request only the teaching style that best suits your child, not mentioning the name of a specific teacher. Some guidelines for parent requests are:

- Put your request in writing.
- Be professional.
- Discuss your child's learning style and needs.
- Understand the school may not be able to accommodate your request.

First Day of School

In the picture book *First Day Jitters* by Julie Danneberg, it is cleverly revealed that both students and the teacher have jitters on the first day of school. At the beginning of a school year, let the relationship between your child and the teacher develop on its own. The first couple of weeks of school are an adjustment period for everyone, as routines are established and relationships are formed. As for your opinion of your child's teacher, base this on your own dealings with the teacher, taking into consideration what your child has to say. Avoid jumping to conclusions and be wary of neighborhood gossip. You would not want the teacher to prejudge your child, so give the teacher the same courtesy.

School Holidays and Professional Development Days

Most school districts have standardized holidays for all their schools. These include a long summer holiday, winter break, spring break (March Break in some areas) and national statutory holidays. Check your school website or newsletter for more information.

School districts usually schedule professional development days (sometimes called professional activity days or staff development days and early release days) for teachers at intervals during the school year. Teachers are involved in report card writing or workshops for new initiatives.

Standardized Testing

Students often write tests in the classroom at the end of a unit of study to evaluate their knowledge. These tests are usually designed by the classroom teacher or grade level teachers. In addition, each state or province has standardized tests administered to students in specific grade levels. A standardized test is the same test delivered and scored in the same manner to a group of students. The original purpose of standardized testing was to improve education and to ensure accountability in the school system by showing that standards are being met. Many people use test results to compare and rank schools and, as a result, there is controversy surrounding these tests.

It is the expectation that children in public schools will write the standardized tests. Children with special needs and English language learners are usually exempt. In some school districts, parents have the right for their child to opt out. Some private schools and home schools may not be required to administer standardized tests.

School Safety

For the safety of everyone in the school, there are mandated classroom and school-wide practices for the following:

- **Fire drill:** an exercise to train students how to vacate the school building quickly and safely in case of fire
- **School evacuation:** an exercise to train students how to vacate the school building quickly and safely in case of gas leak, bomb threat, etc.
- **Lockdown:** an exercise to keep students safe and secure inside the classroom and to keep intruders out. For example, if there has been a robbery in the area and the robber has not been apprehended, the school may be locked down.

Many schools have a security system whereby a person entering the school must ring a doorbell, announce themselves, be seen on camera by someone in the office and "buzzed" into the school. All visitors must report directly to the office, and visitors or parent volunteers in the school must wear a badge or sticker indicating that they are visiting. In some schools, teachers wear photo identification cards on lanyards or clipped to their clothing.

For the safety of students, it has become commonplace in most schools to require volunteers to complete a criminal background check conducted by local police. Getting a background check involves filling out an information form. A fee may be required, which may be covered by the school. School staff members are also required to follow this protocol. Check with your school for details.

Safety in the Schoolyard

All schools have well-established expectations for schoolyard behavior. There are teachers on yard duty at every recess. In some schools, the teachers on duty wear bright safety vests so they can easily be located by students. There are rules governing specific areas of the schoolyard—for example, children may be divided by grade level with younger children in a separate area of the yard from older students.

Prohibited Items

Most schools have a list of items that students are not allowed to bring with them to school. These include any or all of the following: cell phones, cameras, personal entertainment devices, skateboards, alcohol, cigarettes and drugs. The school policy on prohibited items will be communicated to you in a newsletter or on the school website.

Extracurricular Activities

Most schools offer a variety of extracurricular activities that may include sports and clubs run by teacher or parent volunteers. There is usually no cost to students who take part in sports-related extracurricular activities. Sometimes there is a fee for materials, for example, for a knitting or ceramics club.

It's a great idea for all kids to get involved in an extracurricular activity in an area of interest. For some school sports teams, students must try out and be chosen for the team. Many schools also offer in-school (intramural) sports that any student can sign up for and enjoy.

Parent Involvement

Volunteer organizations such as a Parent-Teacher Association (PTA), Parent-Teacher Organization (PTO), Parent Council, School Advisory Council or School Council are made up of parents, teachers and school staff. These organizations have a charter that outlines policies and regulations and the roles and responsibilities of executive members and committees and their functions. Their goals are to support and enhance the educational experience of all the children in the school, organize school events, encourage parent involvement and raise funds for extra educational resources and programs. Joining the volunteer organization for your school enables you to meet and network with other parents, know first-hand the issues of importance to the school, have input into setting goals for the school and join the executive or a committee.

You can attend meetings and volunteer your services whenever possible. Some of the many ways you could volunteer are:

- hand out pizza or any special lunch food
- read with children
- photocopy
- assist with coaching
- sew costumes
- be a guest speaker
- flip burgers at the school BBQ
- shelve books in the library
- go on class trips
- run an extracurricular club

These volunteer activities are a great way to contribute and get a feel for what's going on in your child's school. Most children are proud and "tickled pink" to see their parent(s) in the school. Some schools have policies that do not allow parents to volunteer in their own child's classroom. Do not be insulted if asked to go to the police for a criminal check. This is commonplace and required for the safety of everyone in the school. You should call the school directly or talk to the secretary, principal or a teacher to see what volunteer jobs are available in the school.

How to Be a Good Parent Volunteer

- Find out the requirements and procedures.
- Be on time and call if you cannot be there.
- Be flexible if you are asked to do something different.
- Make babysitting arrangements for younger siblings.
- Keep information confidential (for example, if you overhear a conversation of a sensitive nature about a student or a teacher).
- Understand that the teacher is busy and may not have time to chat.
- Let the teacher handle any discipline problems.
- Be as helpful as you can, enjoy the students and have fun.

Medical Issues

Before your child enters the school system, you must be sure that his immunizations are up to date. Contact the school or your family doctor for specific requirements. Some states also require a tuberculosis skin test.

If your child has a serious medical condition such as life-threatening allergy, diabetes, epilepsy, HIV or asthma, you should inform the school and provide detailed information about all aspects of your child's health issue. This is another case where you need to be a strong advocate for your child and you may need to educate the educators. Make sure the school understands the particulars of your child's condition: symptoms, treatment, medications, emergency procedures, use of any devices such as a puffer, EpiPen or blood glucose meter. Appropriate documentation will need to be filled out.

Some schools actually have a school nurse on staff. Schools without a nurse usually have several staff members with formal first aid training. All staff members are made aware of students with serious medical conditions and most staffs are trained in the use of EpiPens.

Speak to your child's teacher every year to inform her of your child's condition and if you wish to give an educational talk to the class about your child's condition, or find out if a school nurse, public health nurse or other health care professional is available for that purpose. There are excellent books and educational films on most medical conditions that are suitable for viewing in the classroom. Consult your doctor or local public health professional.

Life-Threatening Allergies

A small percentage of students have life-threatening allergies to peanuts, tree nuts, bee stings, shellfish and other substances. Anaphylaxis is a reaction that occurs when histamines are released into body systems. Symptoms of anaphylaxis can range from hives and swelling to shortness of breath, difficulty swallowing, vomiting and loss of consciousness. The treatment is epinephrine, usually administered through an auto-injector such as an EpiPen.

Many schools promote a "nut free" environment so that all students can be safe. There is a standard protocol in every school district.

Advice from a mom with a peanut-allergic child

There are three key things for a child with a severe allergy to remember:

1. Avoid the allergen.

2. Always have an EpiPen on your person.

3. After injecting an EpiPen call 911. If the emergency happens at school, staff should call 911 even before they call the parents.

Make sure your child understands that there can be absolutely **no sharing of food.** Go over this with your child again and again. No school can ever be 100% nut free.

Write a letter to the parents of the children in your child's class at the beginning of the year (you may wish to speak to the teacher first) with your contact information and suggestions for peanut-free lunch ideas, including a recipe for nut-free granola bars. Encourage them to call you if they have any questions about what is a safe food to send for lunch.

Give the teacher information (books and videos) to educate the class about the allergy.

Other Health Concerns

The importance of hand washing has been highlighted by doctors and in the media. Be sure your child knows how to thoroughly wash and dry his hands.

Instruct your child to cough or sneeze into his elbow and not his hands. Many people are referring to this action as "the Dracula," as it brings to mind Dracula pulling his cape over his face. Young children especially love to do this.

If your child becomes ill or is injured at school, you will be notified. Be sure that the school has a current list of phone numbers where you can be reached, or emergency contacts in case you cannot be reached. In the case of minor falls, scrapes or other "boo-boos," Band-aids and comfort are offered by teachers and/or office staff.

When to Keep Your Child Home from School

The general rule of thumb is that if your child has a fever, very runny nose or bad cough, severe sore throat or earache, diarrhea, vomiting or a contagious disease, he should stay home. Check with your doctor if you need more information.

Legal Issues

It is important that you inform your child's school of any legal or custody issues regarding your child. The school should know which parent has legal custody of the child and if there are any court orders affecting who may see or pick the child up at school.

Inform the school of any special arrangements that need to be made, if for example, a copy of the report card should be sent separately to each parent. If at all possible, parents should try to attend parent-teacher conferences together to show their child that they are both interested and unified in their support of his education. If not possible, make arrangements for two separate interviews.

Child Abuse

If teachers have reasonable cause to believe that one of their students is being abused, they are bound by law to report suspected child abuse or neglect directly to police or a local child protective service agency.

It takes a lot of people and procedures to organize a school so that it runs smoothly.

- Many types of professionals make up a school staff
- Students are placed in classes based on multiple factors
- Some schools accept parent input for class placement
- Safety procedures are practiced school-wide
- There are many extracurricular activities for students to enjoy
- Parents can get involved by volunteering or joining the parent committee
- There are procedures to follow for medical and legal situations

Chapter 4

Early Learning, Reading and Writing Development

One of the goals of education is to produce lifelong learners—and it starts early. From the time our children are born, we are amazed at their leaps-and-bounds learning. Our babies learn to hold their head up, they smile and respond to our voices. They discover their hands, hold a bottle on their own, roll over, sit up, stand up and suddenly they are not babies any more.

As parents, we foster and facilitate a child's learning by doing what comes naturally. We talk, share stories, name objects in books and in the world, color and draw pictures, sing, play and laugh with our child. Through these everyday activities at home, young children learn new words, ask and answer questions, retell familiar stories and experiences, explore and learn about themselves and the world around them, interact socially with other people, follow directions and experience happiness. All of these things lay the groundwork for more formal learning, especially in reading and writing.

Balanced Literacy

At school, the literacy program in a good primary classroom will devote time to each of the following areas:

- language (speaking, listening, phonological awareness, phonemic awareness, phonics)
- reading
- writing

Here is an overview of what is taught in each of these areas in primary classrooms.

Language

What Is Done at School

Speaking skills: Vocabulary development, turn taking, appropriate tone of voice, eye contact, adapting to different audiences and topics.

Listening skills: Active listening, focusing on and paying attention to the speaker, not interrupting, interpreting tone of voice, understanding and being able to recall one-, two- or three-step directions.

Phonological awareness: Hearing, identifying and producing (speaking) aspects of spoken language such as rhyming words, syllables, alliteration.

Phonemic awareness: Hearing, identifying, isolating and manipulating individual sounds in spoken language, for example, cat =/c/ /a/ /t/. Take away the /c/ and substitute /b/ and you get bat.

Phonics: Understanding the letter-sound relationship in printed text, for example, the child prints a 'd' under a picture of a dog.

What You Can Do at Home

- Practice the art of conversation. Teach your child to be a good listener, to make eye contact, not to interrupt, to take turns, to stay on topic, to use appropriate volume and tone of voice, to ask and answer questions.
- Model good conversation etiquette yourself.
- Give your child one-, then two-, then three-step directions to follow.
- Clap out the syllables in names and words with your child.
- Read alphabet books together, pointing out, naming and making the sounds of the letters.
- Ask your child to identify letters she sees on signs, books, cereal boxes or anywhere you see letters.
- Read books and sing songs with rhymes in them.
- Play word games, for example, say a word sound-by-sound and have your child figure out the word: "It is /h/ /o/ /t/."
- Play with the initial sounds in words and names: change "Lara" to "Bara," "Para" or "Cara."
- Play "I Spy" with sounds: "I spy something that starts with the sound /b/."

Reading

What Is Done at School

Reading to students (read alouds): When the teacher reads aloud, it's enjoyable, exposes children to a wide variety of literature, provides modeling of good reading, develops vocabulary and story sense, and provides motivation to learn to read.

Reading with students (shared reading): The teacher conducts a lesson with a small or whole class group focusing on enjoying the book (often a "Big Book," which is a large book that is usually rested on an easel and read by the teacher). The focus is also on teaching the strategies good readers use, such as predicting, elements of a story (characters, setting, plot, sequence), directionality (reading top to bottom, left to right), punctuation, distinguishing between types of texts (fiction, nonfiction, poetry) etc.

Reading by students (guided reading): Usually done in groups of four to six students who are at the same reading level and are all reading a copy of the same book. An instructional lesson is given and reading skills are taught; the teacher listens to each child read. (Typically the children read at their own pace and the teacher moves from one student to another, not "round robin" as in the old days.) Students are encouraged to use cueing systems (meaning, structure, visual) when reading.

Reading by students (independent reading): Children are free to choose their own books and other classroom reading materials (books from previous guided reading sessions, class library books, Big Books, charts, magazines). They read alone or with a partner. Students enjoy self-selecting materials, exploring them, talking about them and sharing them with others.

Cueing Systems in Reading

Children are taught to use several strategies when decoding an unfamiliar word. They use their knowledge to make an "educated guess." The three main cueing systems are:

1. **Meaning (semantic):** Does it make sense? Children make use of prior knowledge and their own experiences plus context clues.
2. **Structure (syntactic):** Does it sound right? Children use their knowledge of language and the way it should sound.
3. **Visual (graphophonic):** Does it look right? Children use their knowledge of letter/sound relationships, break words down into letters, sounds and parts.

Other reading strategies include:
- Looking at the picture (which is very important in early reading)
- Skip the word and keep going
- Read the word or sentence again
- Look for familiar small words or parts of words in a larger word
- Ask for help

Children are encouraged to try as many strategies as they can on their own before asking for help.

Sight Words

Sight words are words that children learn to read "on sight," that is, without decoding. Many sight words have irregular spelling patterns that are difficult to sound out, so they are learned whole. A child's first sight word is usually her name. In the classroom, sight words are often posted on a "Word Wall," which is used for language activities and student reference when writing. Practicing sight words at home can give your child more confidence when learning to read.

Common first sight words: **a, and, big, can, come, for, go, here, I, in, is, it, jump, little, look, make, me, my, of, play, said, saw, see, that, the, to, up, was, we, where, you.**

Other early sight words include color words and names of family members and friends.

Trivia fact: In the 1950s, a man named Theodor Geisel wrote a book that used 223 words from a list of easy words children learn at school. The result was *The Cat in the Hat* and Geisel is better known to us today as Dr. Seuss.

What You Can Do at Home

- Read to and with your child every day and spend time talking about books you have read together.
- Talk about the differences between letters and words.
- Point out that we read from left to right and top to bottom.
- Talk about punctuation marks.
- Make connections between things you have read in books and situations in your own life, things in the world, things in other books.
- Let your child "read" to you by telling the story from the pictures in a book.
- Work on identifying letters of the alphabet and their sounds.
- Have a variety of reading materials available.
- Read everything around you: cereal boxes, street signs, calendars.
- If your child is having difficulty with reading or writing, ask your doctor to check her hearing and vision.
- Praise your child's efforts. (Children who believe they can read are more likely to be reading for real in a shorter time.)

Make Reading Fun

- You can make a huge difference in your child's literacy life by reading to her and talking about everything.
- Parents contribute to reading success in ways that school cannot. Snuggle reading, plenty of one-to-one time, a lifetime of favorite shared stories and books — all of these things can only happen between a parent and child.
- Making connections is crucial. When you talk, model and get your child to make these kinds of connections: text to text (comparing one book to another), text to self (connection between the book and herself), text to world (connection between a book and a real life event).
- Strike a balance between reading for pleasure and reading lessons with your child.
- Memorization is an important stage in learning to read. If, while reading, your child is reciting words that are clearly memorized, it's okay. She will soon progress to reading the words on her own.
- Picture cues are very important in early reading. Allow your child to use the picture to figure out the words.
- In early reading, children often read pattern books, which provide short, predictable sentences that a child can read by using the pattern, the pictures and early reading strategies, for example: I can run. I can jump. I can sing.
- If your child cannot decode a word, tell her the word after a try or two. If she becomes frustrated, she will lose the thread of the story and the joy of reading. This stage lasts only a little while and then she will be able to decode almost every word independently.

Boys

For many years people have talked about the fact that boys are often slower than girls when learning to read, and they are less interested in reading than girls. But recent studies have found that given the right materials, boys are drawn in to reading, become engrossed in the material and they will keep on reading as their skills improve. Many boys prefer nonfiction reading materials, audiobooks or nontraditional formats such as comics, graphic novels and magazines. Bathroom humour is especially, although not exclusively, popular with boys: witness the success of the *Captain Underpants* books. Check out author Jon Scieszka's great website, "Guys Read" (www.guysread.com).

Reading at Home: Business or Pleasure?

When you and your young child read together at home, the majority of the reading you do should be for pure pleasure and love of reading. When you work on reading instruction, keep it light, keep it positive and keep the sessions short. Ask your child's teacher for suggestions of books at her reading level.

When you work on reading instruction at home:

- Choose a time when both you and your child are in a relaxed frame of mind.
- Talk about the cover of the book and the cover illustration. Use the words "title," "author" and "illustrator" as you look at the words on the cover.
- Do a "picture walk" before you read by looking at, and talking about, the pictures on each page of the book and not reading the words. Make predictions and talk about what is happening in the pictures. This will help your child predict what words are likely to be in the book. For instance, if the story is about a baseball game, she knows that the words "bat," "ball" and "run" will likely be in the book.
- Teach one-to-one matching by having your child point to the words as she reads.

Be patient with your child as she experiments with reading and encourage her efforts.

Magnetic Letters

Many families work with magnetic letters on the refrigerator. (Magnets will not stick to some stainless steel appliances. In that case, use a small magnet board.)

- Have your child make her name with the letters. Write the names of family members on cards and have her make those names with the magnetic letters.
- Sort the letters by color, shape of letter (for example, those that are round, those that are straight, those that have both a round and a straight part), letters that have a part that points up and those that have a part that points down.
- Match upper and lower case letters.
- Make messages on the fridge with the letters, read them to your child and have her "read" them to you.

- Have your child pick a letter, say its name and sound, and then find something in the house that starts with that letter and sound.
- Make a simple word such as "at." Ask your child what letter she should put at the beginning to make the word "cat," "bat," "mat" and "sat." Repeat with other words and letters.
- Ask your child to pick five letters and print them on a piece of paper.

Writing

What Is Done at School

Writing for students (shared writing): The teacher works with a group of students to write a group story or message. The teacher does the writing, models and gives lessons on directionality, letter formation, stretching out a word verbally and writing the sounds, what is a word, sentences, punctuation, spaces between words and the group reads back what the teacher has written.

Writing with students (interactive writing): A group exercise composing a text. The teacher and students "share the pen" (children take turns writing a word, part of a word or a single letter). The emphasis is on hearing the individual sounds in words, using print resources in the classroom (a child could copy a word from the Word Wall or a word posted somewhere in the room). All students are able to contribute at their own level.

Writing by students (independent writing): Students write on their own, are able to practice the skills learned in shared and interactive writing sessions, draw a picture and write a story or labels, stretch out words orally and write the sounds they hear. The teacher will listen to the student read back what they have written and give individualized instruction.

What You Can Do at Home

- Have a variety of writing materials available for your child to use.
- Let your child see you writing lists, notes, etc.
- Use sidewalk chalk to make letters and write notes.
- Teach your child the proper way to grip a pencil (see Chapter 1).
- Work on printing letters of the alphabet and words.
- Work with your child to make signs and labels to post in your home.

- Have your child draw pictures and then write a story and read it back to you. (Even if your child can't really write she will be able to "read" back the scribbles or letters she has written.)
- Teach your child to write on paper from top to bottom and left to right.
- Encourage your child to say words slowly as she writes, and to write the sounds she hears.
- Have your child write and illustrate a menu and name cards for your evening meal and place them on the table for the family to read.
- It is difficult for children to do in writing what they have not done orally, so make sure your home is filled with conversation, songs and story telling.
- Praise your child for any and all efforts in writing. Hearing "Wow, you are a writer," can help your child believe that she really is writing and help motivate her to keep trying.

Invented Spelling

When young children begin to write, they generally write the letter that matches the sound they hear. Sometimes, they do not hear all the sounds in a word and will write things like "cde" for "candy." Usually, the initial consonant is the first one they can identify, followed by the final consonant and then the middle sounds and vowels.

Parents are sometimes concerned about invented spelling (sometimes called inventive spelling) and the fact that teachers are encouraging their students to spell words in unconventional ways.

The theory behind invented spelling is to encourage and free the child to write independently, and to write a sentence or story concentrating on the message, not the mechanics of what she is writing. It was never meant to be "anything goes." Invented spelling helps children to develop their understanding of how sounds make up words.

When young children write "b" for "button," "pk" for "park" or "pla" for "play," teachers and parents need to respond, "Good writing! I can read that!" or "You got the first letter!" (or "last letter" or "most of the sounds").

If young children are asked to write only the words they know how to spell correctly, they will stop taking risks and limit what they write only to the words they are sure of. When they are free to write what they hear, they produce imaginative stories and delightful narratives.

Practicing the sounds of the letters in a casual way at home and during family activities is a good way to build on the work that is done at school and to increase your child's confidence when writing. Be assured that in time, invented spelling gives way to conventional (if not perfect) spelling. Also keep in mind that writing skills are developmental and that each child passes through the stages at her own pace, just as they do for crawling, walking, speaking and potty training.

Some of our favorite invented spellings from our students over the years include "comba" for coma (this child understood silent letters), "myoczm" for museum and "roll mottle" for role model. Then there was the child who was looking at the letter "z." When she was asked: "What sound does this letter make?" she responded, "Sleep." One sweet little kindergarten girl who was still working on distinguishing letters from numbers once asked: "How many zeroes are in 'zoo'?"

Reversals

Many parents are concerned about letter and number reversals in their young child's writing. The most commonly reversed letters are "b" and "d," "p" and "q." Reversals do not necessarily indicate a learning problem. Many young children reverse letters and numbers when they are first learning to write. In most cases, this is a developmental stage and will right itself in time. Check with your child's teacher if you are concerned. You can help by teaching a memory trick such as: "b" is the first letter in baseball. The stick on the letter "b" looks like a baseball bat. The round part of the letter "b" looks like a ball. You have to have a bat before you can hit the ball, so the stick comes before the ball part in letter "b." For the letter "d," teach your child that the letter "d" is the first letter in dog. The round part of the letter "d" looks like a dog's body. The stick looks like a tail. The body comes first, then the tail goes at the end.

Development Stages of Writing

Scribbles Child understands that writing has meaning

Random letters Child has some knowledge of letters

Random letters or scribbles with gaps Child has some knowledge of words

Initial consonants Child is hearing the first letter in words

I L P (I like popsicles.)

Initial and final consonants Child is hearing first and last letters in words

plr (park) dg (dog)

Middle sounds Child is hearing all sounds in words

bi gr (bigger) Ladr (ladder)

Spelling approaches standard

I luv Mom ond dod

Child's ability to hear sounds in words and knowledge about conventional spelling are coming together

The Ball and Stick

Most letters of the alphabet are made up of circles and straight lines teachers call balls and sticks. When printing a letter, children should form the letter from left to right and from top to bottom. The ball should be printed counterclockwise and the stick should go from the top down.

Getting a good start in literacy begins at home. Early literacy experiences at home lay the foundation for reading and writing in the classroom.

- Classrooms use a balanced literacy approach covering language (listening and speaking), reading and writing
- There are many ways you can help your child at home in all of these areas
- Reading and writing are developmental and children progress at their own pace

Chapter 5

Ways Children Learn

Children are amazing. When they are young, they learn at a ferocious rate and seem to take in information through every pore of their bodies. They use all their senses and they have fun. It has been our experience in the classroom that kids learn better when they are encouraged and inspired. Educators have learned to recognize the strengths and learning styles of their students and to teach in a way that brings out their strengths and supports their areas of weakness.

Learning is not always easy and natural. Whether it is a young child struggling with early reading or an older child wrestling with integers, there are times when learning can be frustrating. At such times, it is a matter of identifying the problem area, explaining, re-teaching in a different way and lots and lots of practice. Another key is keeping the child's attitude positive by encouraging his efforts and giving honest, but not overdone, praise.

Children, and in fact all of us, think and learn in different ways. Here are several ways in which children learn, the ways that teachers vary their instruction to meet the needs of all students and ways parents can support different learning styles at home.

Modeling

One of the first ways children learn is through modeling. They observe the actions of another person and imitate what they see. The most influential models in a child's early life are the members of their family. When children observe the gestures, tone of voice and actions of family members, they store the information and will often mimic what they have seen and heard. For example, they will pretend to be stirring a pot, rocking a baby or driving a car. Children learn many skills through modeling, such as brushing their teeth, holding and reading a book, and setting the table. When they start school, children model themselves after the teacher. How many times have you heard your child say, "My teacher says… ."

Play

When children play, they are taking what they have seen and heard, using their imaginations to act it out. When Laura taught kindergarten, she found that one of the best ways of assessing student learning was to watch children play. Through play, the children demonstrated their understanding of freshly learned concepts. For example, when studying animals in winter, there was a lot of play with animal puppets and plastic animals and a lot of talk about different animals that hibernate, how animals prepare for winter, changes of seasons and waking up in the springtime. Through play, children develop gross and fine motor skills, interaction with others, vocabulary, problem-solving skills and creativity.

Three Basic Learning Styles

Visual learners (learning through seeing): Visual learners think in pictures and learn best from visual displays such as watching the teacher's gestures and expression, reading maps, diagrams, charts, illustrations, videos, work sheets and essays. These learners gather information by reading books.

Auditory learners (learning through hearing): Auditory learners learn best through talking, listening to the input of others and discussions. Written information has more meaning once it has been heard. Reading aloud or using a tape recorder helps these learners absorb information.

Tactile or kinesthetic learners (learning through touching, doing and moving): Tactile learners learn best through a hands-on approach and by actively exploring and experiencing. These are the "doers" and they enjoy model building, discovery and action. They learn through imitation and practice.

Some children fall into two categories at the same time.

Multiple Intelligences

In 1983, Howard Gardner developed the theory of multiple intelligences, which essentially describes the eight different ways people learn. The eight intelligences are:
- Verbal / Linguistic Intelligence (Word Smart)
- Logical / Mathematical Intelligence (Number Smart)
- Musical/ Rhythmic Intelligence (Music Smart)
- Bodily / Kinesthetic Intelligence (Body Smart)
- Visual / Spatial Intelligence (Picture Smart)
- Intrapersonal Intelligence (Self Smart)
- Interpersonal Intelligence (People Smart)
- Naturalist Intelligence (Nature Smart)

Children can have more than one area of strength among the eight intelligences. Without even knowing who Howard Gardner is, you will know early on what types of intelligences are strengths that your child has. Betty's daughter, Kate, sang a lot as a kid, loved to draw, do crafts and play dress up. It was no surprise that Kate ended up in a school for the arts, and sang, danced and acted her way through high school.

Bloom's Taxonomy

Benjamin Bloom was an American educational psychologist who classified levels of thinking in the 1950s. He identified six levels of thinking and organized them by level of complexity. Bloom's levels of thinking were updated in 2001 by Anderson and Krathwohl to add relevancy for twenty-first-century teachers and students.

In each grade, teachers work to move children up the levels of thinking. Even a kindergarten child can create and evaluate. The levels of thinking (starting with the lowest) are:
- Remembering: recalling, retrieving, identifying
- Understanding: describing, summarizing, explaining
- Applying: implementing, carrying out, demonstrating
- Analyzing: taking apart, examining, comparing
- Evaluating: judging, critiquing, assessing
- Creating: planning, generating, producing

How Teachers Teach to Reach the Learning Needs of All Students

In the classroom, teachers must take into account the different learning styles of their students when planning lessons, activities and methods of assessment. Teachers use differentiated instruction, which means that a variety of strategies and methods are used. There are a number of ways teachers individualize and tailor instruction:
- Providing choice for students: The culminating activity for a novel study could be a written response journal, a skit, an oral presentation or a song.
- Having a range of materials to suit the individual needs of the students: Fiction and nonfiction books, concrete materials, posters, educational films, etc.

- Making use of graphic organizers: Using Venn diagrams, cycle of events charts, and story webs.
- Building in movement: Movement break between written activities, role play or acting out.
- Allowing for extra practice: Using a computer game to provide extra practice in a skill.
- Using tiered instruction: All students studying the same topic are divided into groups based on their learning needs, readiness or interest. Each group is given an assignment tailored—or tiered— to meet the needs of the group members.
- Flexible grouping: Just because your child is in the Buzzards reading group doesn't mean they will always be in the same group.
- Cooperative learning: Students work together in pairs and groups.
- Direct instruction: A teacher-led lesson is taught, perhaps a song. Students repeat each line after the teacher and practice the song together.
- Inquiry based learning: Based on discovering answers to student questions. Students brainstorm a list of questions on a topic and set out to find the answers through research.

How Parents Can Help Children Learn at Home

- Being aware that you are modeling for your child in what you do and say (children copy what they see and hear)
- Providing plenty of free play time for young children
- Providing leisure time for older children (don't overschedule)
- Identifying which of the three learning styles is strongest for your child. (Speak to your child's teacher about her learning at school. Use this information when you teach your child a skill or work with her on schoolwork.)
- Providing a variety of experiences for your child to appeal to all her senses, to expose her to various types of learning and to interest her in different ways of taking in information
- Engaging your child's thinking skills by asking higher level questions such as: Can you describe… ? How is… related to… ? What are the parts of… ? What do you think about… ? Do you agree that… ?

- Working with your child on activities that use the different ways of learning
- Talking a lot with your child. (Get her to talk about thoughts and feelings and to ask questions. Talk about experiences you have together and those she has while at school or in someone else's care. Talk about everything.)

Children learn in many different ways beginning at home with modeling and playing. By exposing them to many learning experiences it becomes evident what type of learner they are.

Teachers provide differentiated instruction to meet the needs of various types of learners.

Parents can support learning by:
- Exposing children to many different learning experiences
- Asking questions that promote higher level thinking
- Ongoing conversation about everything and anything

Chapter 6

Reading to and with Your Child

Reading to and with your child is probably the single most important thing you can do to help him be successful in school. And, as Dr. Seuss would say, "Oh the places you'll go!" When you read with your baby, you are helping him take his first steps toward becoming a reader and a literate person. A traditional definition of literacy is the ability to read and write. In recent years, this definition has been broadened to include understanding and interpreting text, critical thinking, expressing ideas and opinions, problem solving, decision-making and processing information. Reading is the key to all of these skills, and it begins in your home as soon as your child is born.

Talking and Literacy

Talk, talk, talk. Just talking all the time is also essential to literacy. When talking to your baby or young child, simply talk about what you are doing and thinking. Point out and name objects. Use simple sentences and phrases and speak with expression, changing the pitch, tone and volume of your voice. This does not mean speaking "baby talk," though every parent loves doing so on occasion. As your child grows, he will begin to respond, at first with coos and noises, and eventually with words.

As your child continues growing, continue talking. Tell family stories, talk about your day, ask questions and wonder aloud. Talk about what's in the news, TV shows and movies. Encourage your child to talk about his day and about anything and everything. Listen to what he has to say. Conversation is an important building block for literacy development.

When to Start Reading to Your Child

Children can be read to from the time they are very young. Babies may not understand the story but they recognize the sound of your voice, the warmth of your touch and the intonation of your words. Sharing stories is not limited to reading from a book. Singing a song, repeating a rhyme, telling or retelling a story or just talking helps them unlock the magical world of literacy.

Sharing a book is a natural springboard for conversation. Set aside some time every day for reading to and with your child. Many families choose bedtime because reading is a lovely way to unwind by curling up, enjoying a story and ending the day. You might not even realize that when you read together you are teaching and your child is learning. He is learning in an informal, relaxed and unstructured way.

Kids learn by seeing and doing, so your reading habits will greatly influence them. They will model themselves after you. Our young friend Patrick takes the sports section of the newspaper to school every day because his uncle takes the business section to work with him every day. Don't worry if you are not a strong reader. Just let your child see you reading. Any kind of reading sets a good example. It could be an instruction manual, library book, recipe, newspaper, article on the computer, novel, magazine, something in another language, rules to a board game, textbook, old book, new book, red book, blue book.

Read What You Can

If you are not a strong reader, read what you can manage. Ask a friend or relative to read to your child as well. If English is not your first language, let your child see you reading materials in your own language. Share books in your language with your child.

Reading Routines

In the classroom, there is time set aside for individual quiet reading and reading stories together. There is a routine for reading at school. It is a habit, and something the children look forward to. Try to make reading a routine and a habit in your home, so that losing yourself in a book becomes second nature. Here are some suggestions:

- Set aside at least 15 minutes a day for reading, or a longer time if your child is older.
- Establish a set time, such as before going to sleep or whatever time works for you.
- If you and your child are very absorbed in the story and can't put the book down, just keep reading.
- For younger children, reading several times a day for a shorter time may be better than one longer session.
- Find a comfortable spot and create a quiet, inviting atmosphere with no distractions such as television or music.
- Teach your child to handle books with care.

- Have a special place for books, both your own and library books. This saves the mad scurry and search on the due date.
- Give books to mark special occasions. Write the date and an inscription.
- Be flexible. There will be days when there is no time for reading and that is okay. There will be rainy days when there is all the time in the world to read.
- When traveling, take along some books. If you are going to the beach, take along a story about the beach or a nonfiction book about the seashore. While you are away, visit a local bookstore and if possible purchase a book that has a story that is set in the area or has anything to do with your trip.
- Know when to stop. If it is tough slogging, try another time.

"Read it again!"

Children love to hear the same story over and over and over. The repetition may drive you crazy at times, but kids love what they love and feel safe with what is familiar to them. Indulge them, and know that repeated readings are helping them process all that they are hearing.

A Head Start

Teachers can tell in the first week of school which kids have been read to at home. Children who have had a lot of exposure to books begin school with an advantage. These children have a head start because they:

- can hold a book properly
- have a better vocabulary
- ask more and better questions
- can sit still and focus on the story
- use longer sentences and express themselves more clearly
- make predictions
- read with expression
- can make connections (text to self, text to text and text to world)
- have a more vivid imagination
- become immersed in stories
- are able to think critically

There is also a direct link to writing. Children who have been read to are generally better writers, more sophisticated in their outlook and in possession of a more developed "author's voice." While enjoying books with your child, without even trying, you have given them the desire to read, as well as the foundations for lifelong literacy.

Different Ways of Reading

Read to your child out loud	Your child "reads" to you out loud.	Your child reads out loud.
Change voice when reading.	Take turns reading out loud.	Read out loud to your child. Stop reading and let the child fill in the next word.
You read out loud, substitute a rhyming word, or say the wrong and wait for a correction.	Read out loud together.	Read the same thing together but silently.
Read together silently but each read your own book.	Have an older sibling read to a younger one and vice versa.	Your child reads quietly and you make dinner.

Keep Reading with Them Even When They're Big Kids

Keep reading to and with your child even when he can read on his own — even when he becomes taller than you. Some older children will become avid readers, happy to read on their own, and some will fall away from reading in their teen years. Keep encouraging them, offer them reading materials you think might engage them and keep being a good reading role model. Chances are, they will come back to reading at some point.

One way to keep older children discussing books with you is to parallel read. Read the same book as your child or a different book by the same author or an adult book on the same topic. Compare notes with your child and see where the conversation takes you.

Talking About Books

Talking about books is almost as important as reading them. Before you read a book, while you are reading a book and after you have read a book, talk, talk, talk. It's all about making connections with personal experiences, with other books you have read and with the world around you. Making connections helps your child fully understand the story.

Ways to talk about books:
- "Go with the flow," go off on tangents and let the conversation take flight.
- Engage your child in discussion about the book. If you ask "Did you like the book?" you will get either "Yes" or "No" for an answer and the conversation will be over. Try asking questions such as "Who was your favorite character? Tell me why?" "What made you laugh?" (or sad, mad, surprised) "What was your favorite part of the book?" "What did you notice?"
- Share and discuss favorite books from your own childhood.
- Study and comment on the illustrations as there is often a lot going on in the pictures that isn't in the text.
- Encourage your child to make predictions after looking at the front cover and during the story.
- Think out loud about what is going through your head while you are reading, and encourage your child to do the same and to ask questions.
- Compare and contrast characters, settings, plots, solutions and endings with other books and experiences.

Choosing Books

There are literally thousands of fabulous books for your child to choose from. To some extent, your child will be influenced by what the teacher is reading to the class, what friends are reading, what's "hot" and her own personal preferences. If your child is looking for additional recommendations, bookstores and libraries have displays and lists of highly recommended books. Public librarians, school librarians and teachers are always happy to help out and give suggestions. The books that are featured in school book club flyers are age and reading-level appropriate, and they are great reads. You and your child can also go online to check out award-winning titles, as well as find out what's new, the best books of the year, books every child should know, must-reads and all-time favorites. Look for books that have won literary awards such as the Newbery Medal, Caldecott Medal, Coretta Scott King Award or the Governor-General's Award.

Other ways for a child to choose an appropriate book include:

- Knowing his own reading level. If in doubt, he should ask the teacher. Not every child reads exactly at grade level. Children can be reading below, at or above their grade level
- Reading the blurb on the back cover to see if the book appeals
- Reading, understanding and liking the first page of a book
- Persevering and keeping in mind that it might take a chapter or two to "get into" the book
- Checking the reading level that is sometimes printed on the back cover or on the back of the title page (for example: R.L. 3.5 means Reading Level Grade 3.5)
- Revisiting old favorites

The Five-Finger Rule

At school, children are taught how to figure out if a book is at their reading level. When a seven-year-old kid tries to sign out *War and Peace*, we encourage him to use the "five-finger rule." The child picks a page with a lot of text and starts reading. Each time he comes across a word he cannot read, he holds up a finger. If five fingers are up before the end of the page, the book is too difficult and beyond his reading level. If no fingers are up, the book may be too easy, but can be used for reading fluency practice. If two or three fingers are up, the book is at the child's instructional level.

Building a Home Library

It is ideal to have a varied collection of age-appropriate books in your home. There are many different ways to build a home library:

- Buy new books.
- Buy used books (at tag sales or garage sales).
- Ask for books as birthday and Christmas gifts.
- Subscribe to a children's magazine.
- Trade books with other families.
- Shop at school book fairs. (The proceeds of these sales usually benefit the school library.)
- Order through classroom book clubs. (Teachers distribute flyers and place the orders and receive free books for the classroom based on sales.)

You can also have a collection of books in your home on loan from the public library or the school library. Familiarize yourself with the neighborhood library and get to know the librarians. Being surrounded by books and enveloped in a warm quiet atmosphere can be comforting and inspiring. How excited your child will be to have a library card with his very own name on it. Be very careful to return the borrowed materials on time, or you will face the wrath of "Conan the Librarian" and possibly a fine.

What a Library Has to Offer

The library (not "liberry" as the kids say) has hundreds of thousands of books available to borrow for free. In addition, the library has other materials (for children and adults) available for loan, including video games, DVDs, CDs, audio books, magazines, and sometimes mp3 files and e-books. The librarians are experts in recommending books and helping your child find research materials. Here are some other programs that many libraries offer:

- Free programs such as story time, summer and school break reading programs, book clubs, guest speakers and exhibitions
- Special "reader participation" programs. (Children read a selection of books from a set list and vote for their favorite. An award is presented to the author of the winning book. Some well-known programs of this type include Forest of Reading in Ontario, Canada; Texas Bluebonnet Awards; California's Young Reader Medal Program; and the Pacific Northwest Library

Association's Young Reader's Choice Award, which has been going strong since 1940. School libraries often participate.)
- Computer and Internet access, as well as direction in using them
- Homework help through the children's reference section
- Local event recommendations, calendars and pamphlets
- Free family passes to museums, art galleries and historical sites
- Online access to the entire library collection including item requests and renewals
- Library websites contain links to games, audio books, contests, online animated storybooks, encyclopedias and online databases

What Your Child Learns from Reading Different Types of Books

Board or cloth books: This type of book can handle independent holding, enthusiastic page turning, drooling and biting and gives your baby a taste for books. Some of our favorites are:
>*Goodnight Moon* by Margaret Wise Brown
>*Time for Bed* by Mem Fox
>*Jamberry* by Bruce Degen
>*The Very Hungry Caterpillar* by Eric Carle
>*Brown Bear Brown Bear* by Bill Martin Jr.

Nursery rhymes, finger plays, songs and Mother Goose: Even though you probably know many songs and rhymes by heart, it's also good to have them in print form. Having the book fosters questioning about the text and discussion about the illustrations. For example: "Did you know that Humpty Dumpty was an egg?" Having a book in your hand gives you a wonderful opportunity to help your child begin to discover that those funny little marks are letters and strung together, they are words. Some suggestions are:
>*Favorite Nursery Rhymes From Mother Goose*
>>illustrated by Scott Gustafson
>*A Child's Treasury of Nursery Rhymes*
>>by Kady MacDonald Denton
>*Hand Rhymes* collected by Marc Brown
>Any of the *Raffi Songs to Read* books by Raffi
>*Children's Song Bag* by Paul DuBois Jacobs

Environmental print: At home and in the community, signs, symbols, logos, labels, words on packaging, computer icons and billboard advertising are considered environmental print. Children are quick to learn and remember these highly visual everyday kind of prints. They can spot their favorite restaurant from a mile away. Being able to recognize the sign is the first step to reading. The child is beginning to understand that there is meaning in print. When your child recognizes a sign or symbol, this is a great opportunity for you to build him up and say, "Wow, you can read!" We know from experience that a child who believes he can read is much more confident and is more likely to experience early reading success.

ABC and 1-2-3 books: Alphabet, number, color and category books are visual and clever. They help the child learn basic concepts and are a good reference for beginning readers and writers. For babies and toddlers:

> *Chicka Chicka ABC* by Bill Martin Jr.
> *Eating the Alphabet* by Lois Ehlert
> *Big Board Colors, ABC, Numbers (Bright Baby)* by Roger Priddy
> *Ten, Nine, Eight* by Molly Bang
> *Counting Kisses* by Karen Katz

For school-age children:

> *A Was Once an Apple Pie* by Edward Lear illustrated by Suse Macdonald
> *Q Is for Duck* by Mary Elting and Michael Folsom
> *A My Name Is Alice* by Jane E. Bayer
> *Tomorrow's Alphabet* by George Shannon
> *How Do Dinosaurs Count to Ten* by Jane Yolen

Picture books: There is a whole world of beautifully written and illustrated picture books just waiting for you and child to discover. Picture books cover every scenario imaginable such as books with your child's name in them (exciting for your child), stories that make you laugh out loud or bring tears to your eyes, books about real-life situations, such as losing a tooth, picture day at school, moving to a new house, the death of a pet, kinds of hair or hair in funny places, just to name a few.

Don't be limited by the age recommendation on a picture book. Many of them, though targeted at and appropriate for young children, contain subtleties, humor, complexities and subtext that can only be appreciated by an older and more sophisticated mind. Older children often return to previously viewed TV shows or films and take away a new understanding. The same holds true for picture books. Adolescents are growing up, but are at heart, they are "little kids in big bodies" and still enjoy being read to. Favorites tried and true and new:

Anything by Dr. Seuss or Robert Munsch
Any *Curious George* story by H. A. Rey
Any *Arthur* book by Marc Brown
Blueberries for Sal by Robert McCloskey
Any of the *David* books by David Shannon
Any of the *Olivia* books by Ian Falconer
Matthew A.B.C. by Peter Catalanotto
Little Pea by Amy Krouse Rosenthal
Pete's a Pizza by William Steig

Leveled reading books: These are short pattern books with pictures that are reading-level appropriate for children in the early grades. Once the child has mastered a level, he has the confidence and skills to step up to the next level. Leveled books are often used in the classroom for guided reading and are good at home too.

Movable books: Pop-ups, pull-tabs, flaps, pop-outs and pull-downs are considered movable books. They are beautiful, interactive and fragile. Some are designed for little hands, but the very intricate ones are best handled only by you and stored where children cannot reach them. Some really good ones are:

The Jolly Postman by Janet and Alan Ahlberg
How Many Bugs in a Box by David A. Carter
The works of Robert Sabuda
Gallop! By Rufus Butler Seder
One Red Dot by David A. Carter

Novelty books: What kid doesn't love a joke book, sticker book, look-and-find book, drawing book, book that has sound and light or a book that's just plain fun? Here are some suggestions of great novelty books:

Awesome Knock-Knock Jokes for Kids by Bob Phillips
Any Ultimate Sticker Book by DK Publishing
I Can Draw Animals (Usborne Playtime Series) by Ray Gibson
Any *Great Searches* book by Usborne Publishing
The Very Quiet Cricket by Eric Carle

Picture Books for Older Children

There are many picture books designed with both a younger and older audience in mind. Children will "get it" at their own level. There's nothing wrong with older children revisiting and rereading favorite books from years gone by. Often, they will discover new meaning and humor that they didn't "get" the first time around. Here are some excellent books for both younger and older children:

The works of Chris Van Allsburg

The works of Ian Wallace

The works of Jon Scieszka

Robert Sabuda's pop-out books

Somebody and the Three Blairs by Marilyn Tolhurst

Faithful Elephants by Yukio Tsuchiya

The Three Astronauts by Umberto Eco

Cinder Edna by Ellen Jackson

Aunt Harriet's Underground Railroad in the Sky by Faith Ringgold

Martin's Big Words by Doreen Rappaport

Be Boy Buzz by Chris Raschka

The Scary Stories series by Alvin Schwartz

The Man Who Walked between the Towers by Mordecai Gerstein

Folk tales, fairy tales, myths, legends and fables: These are the very rich stories that have been passed down through the generations. Children learn formulas such as "once upon a time," the moral of the story, how things came to be, activities of gods and heroes, and "they all lived happily ever after." Every culture is steeped in these types of stories and you have a great opportunity to share your family's heritage with your children. Some of our favorites are:

Favorite Folktales from around the World by Jane Yolen

A First Book of Fairy Tales by Mary Hoffman

Classic Myths to Read Aloud by William F. Russell

Earth Tales from Around the World by Michael J. Caduto

Aesop's Fables by Anna Milbourne

Classics: Books that have staying power as a result of memorable characters and timeless storylines are considered classics. Sharing an "oldie but goodie" that you enjoyed when you were young is a lovely way to introduce this genre of literature to your child. Many classics have been made into movies. Watching the movie may inspire you and your child to read the book together or vice versa. You may be surprised to find differences between the original story and the movie. For example, in the movie *The Wizard of Oz,* Dorothy's famous shoes were ruby red, but in the book they were actually silver. We suggest reading or watching the movie version of the following:

> *Alice's Adventures in Wonderland* by Lewis Carroll
> *The Wonderful Wizard of Oz* by L. Frank Baum
> *Peter Pan* by J.M. Barrie
> *The Lion, the Witch and the Wardrobe* by C.S. Lewis
> *The Wind in the Willows* by Kenneth Grahame

Chapter and series books: Novels for children fall into several genres including fantasy, science fiction, mystery, adventure, historical fiction, animal stories, humor, growing up and realistic fiction. Your child will probably read a wide range of books and may develop a taste for a certain category or a specific author. Most kids go through a stage where they gobble up one book after another in a series featuring the same characters in every sequel. Favorite tried and true and new chapter books:

> Anything by Roald Dahl
> *Charlotte's Web* by E.B. White
> *Pippi Longstocking* by Astrid Lindgren
> *Bridge to Terabithia* by Katherine Paterson
> *The Indian in the Cupboard* by Lynne Reid Banks
> *Holes* by Louis Sachar
> *The Giver* by Lois Lowry
> *The Tale of Despereaux* by Kate DiCamillo
> *Bud, Not Buddy* by Christopher Paul Curtis

Favorite tried and true and new series books:

> The *Ramona* books by Beverly Cleary
> The *Little House* books by Laura Ingalls Wilder
> The *Silverwing* books by Kenneth Oppel
> The *Magic Treehouse* books by Mary Pope Osborne
> The *Fudge* books by Judy Blume

The *Harry Potter* books by J.K. Rowling
The *Diary of a Wimpy Kid* books by Jeff Kinney
The *Series of Unfortunate Events* books by Lemony Snicket
The *Junie B. Jones* books by Barbara Park
The *Artemis Fowl* books by Eoin Colfer
The *Captain Underpants* books by Dav Pilkey

Comics, graphic novels and magazines: These have become very popular and more accepted as "real reading" than in years gone by. Comics and graphic novels have all the elements of traditional novels, with the bonus of a reader-friendly format, lots of dialogue and cool artwork. Magazines are available on every subject imaginable. Graphic novels for children:

Johnny Boo by James Kochalka
Alia's Mission: Saving the Books of Iraq by Mark Alan Stamaty
Amelia Earhart: Free in the Skies by Robert Burleigh
Dinosaurs across America by Phil Yeh
The Adventures of Tintin by Herge

Popular magazines for children (age levels vary):

The Cricket Magazines: includes *Babybug, Ladybug, Spider* and *Cricket*
The Owl Magazines: includes *Chirp, Chickadee* and *Owl*
The National Geographic magazines: *National Geographic Little Kids* and *National Geographic Kids*
Sports Illustrated Kids (SI Kids)
Kid Crafts Magazine: an online magazine
The Zoobooks Magazines: includes *Zoobies, Zootles* and *Zoobooks*

Nonfiction: This is the largest section of books in any bookstore or library. Nonfiction is where children indulge their interests and read for information. If a child is fascinated with a certain subject, he will devour books that he is able to read well. Kids will also be inclined to jump into books well beyond their reading ability out of sheer love for the subject. Without even knowing it, children will maneuver through the text by reading the captions under the pictures, titles and subtitles, words in bold print or italics, the first and last sentence of a paragraph and skimming the text for details. For example, if a

Books about Real-Life Situations

Many picture books and novels deal with everyday situations that children will face (losing a tooth) or may face in the future (peer pressure). If they read a book on the subject, they are better able to face, handle, understand and relate to the situation. They realize that they are not alone. The book may offer comfort and give direction. Here are some suggestions:

Swimmy by Leo Lionni

Throw Your Tooth on the Roof by Selby Beeler

Spaghetti in a Hot Dog Bun: Having the Courage to Be Who You Are by Maria Dismondy

If Everybody Did by Jo Ann Stover

It's Hard to Be Five by Jamie Lee Curtis

child is highly motivated and interested in dinosaurs, he can usually pick out the word "brontosaurus" even if he is struggling with basic sight words. Some great nonfiction books are:

Any *Eyewitness* Book by DK Publishing

Any *First Discovery* book by Scholastic Publishing

Any *Usborne First Encyclopedia* book by Usborne Publishing

Follow That Map! A First Book of Mapping Skills by Scot Ritchie

A Pinky Is a Baby Mouse by Pam Munoz Ryan

Poetry: Children's poetry can be fun, whimsical and hysterical, or it can be serious and contain a message. A lot of children's poetry is short and snappy, has rhythm and rhyme, and is easy to remember. Poetry plays with language and tells a story in a lyrical, artistic and succinct way. This is another area where you could share a favorite from your youth. We suggest:

Any book by Shel Silverstein

Any book by Dennis Lee

A Family of Poems edited by Caroline Kennedy

Hip Hop Speaks to Children edited by Nikki Giovanni (comes with a CD)

The Random House Book of Poetry for Children edited by Jack Prelutsky

E-books (electronic books): Wave of the future or not? The debate rages on. In the meantime, be aware they are available and give one a try. E-books can be purchased for use on an e-reader. Some e-readers will allow you to download books from the public library. Some books that are in the public domain (the copyright has expired) can be downloaded for free. A good example is *The Wizard of Oz*.

A few features of an e-reader are the device is dead cool, it can store hundreds of books, free chapters are available for preview, there is a feature that reads the story out loud, the font size can be changed and they have built-in dictionaries.

Read for pleasure at home to relax and have fun with your child and to enhance their imagination, vocabulary, self-esteem and knowledge. Sharing books with your child gives him a head start at school and establishes the foundation for lifelong learning.

- Build a collection of books at home
- Set an example by reading
- Read to and with your child
- Choose a variety of reading materials
- Keep on reading as your child gets older
- Discuss the books
- Give your child an advantage at school
- Have fun

Chapter 7

Math and Problem Solving

If literacy is the most important foundation for success at school, then the next most important is numeracy. Numeracy is the cornerstone of mathematics. It is the understanding of numbers, number sense and their related operations, as well as analysis, critical thinking and creating. Numeracy also requires an ability to solve problems.

Young children start learning and making sense of numbers from their early experiences at home and through their everyday life situations. Knowing and using numbers, and carrying out simple operations such as adding, subtracting, multiplying and dividing, begins well before a child starts school. A young child clearly understands how to divide up six candies between three children. As with reading, when you are doing math activities at home, you are informally teaching your child. It is free, fun and effortless and it gives your child an advantage when starting school.

Starting Early

Here are some ideas to help your young child develop math skills. Keep the sessions short, informal and fun.

Counting and Sorting
- Practice skip counting; for example, group items by 2's, 5's and 10's and count them.
- Count down the days until a special occasion like a birthday.
- Help your child count by using everyday household items.
- Sort laundry, money, blocks, cutlery and candy by size, color and shape.

Looking for Numbers
- Point out numbers in books, newspapers and magazines.
- Look for numbers on clocks, TVs, computers, phones and calculators.
- Spot numbers in environmental print, for example, neighborhood signs.
- Have your child learn her house number and telephone number.

Playing Games and Singing Songs
- Sing counting songs.
- Teach number rhymes.

- Play games using dice or cards.
- Choose toys such as blocks for counting and puzzles for problem solving.
- Point out patterns and do patterning activities; for example, when building with LEGO blocks alternate colors.

Using Media

- Use computer programs that bolster math concepts.
- Let your child experiment with a calculator.
- Read books that have a math theme.
- Choose educational TV programs.

Coaching and Encouraging

- Encourage your child to verbalize her thinking while solving a math problem.
- Have a positive attitude toward math, just like the little blue engine that tried so hard to overcome an impossible challenge and kept repeating: "I think I can, I think I can."

Speaking the Language of Math

- Guess and estimate; for example, ask: "How many carrots do you think are in this bunch?"
- Solve simple everyday problems; for example, if there are eight pieces of pizza and four people in your family, how many pieces does each person get?
- Ask questions like: "How much?" "How long?" "How many?"
- Make your child aware of money by teaching the names and value of coins.
- Reinforce math skills through cooking, gardening, grocery shopping, sewing, woodworking and building models.

Using Manipulatives

When your child is first learning to count, help her by pointing to and moving an item as she says each number out loud. Any concrete item will do, such as buttons, Cheerios, macaroni and even her fingers. These items are called manipulatives, as they can be manipulated and moved. They allow the child to explore in an active, hands-on manner.

Manipulatives are very important in the early counting stages. The benefit of using them is that they let the child connect mathematical ideas and symbols to real objects, thereby promoting a better understanding of what's going on. They help the child move from a concrete to an abstract way of thinking.

The concrete stage is the "doing" stage, where the child uses objects to aid in her thinking and to help solve problems. The abstract stage is the "symbolic" stage, where the child uses abstract symbols (numbers and signs) to solve problems. She begins to think abstractly and can mentally visualize what's going on.

At school, math manipulatives have been used in the primary grades for many years and are now incorporated across all grades. They range from counting blocks in kindergarten to the colored tiles required to create complex tessellations (patterns made of identical shapes that fit together without gaps or overlap) in the upper grades.

The 100-Square Chart

There are many math concepts that can be taught and reviewed at home using a 100-square chart, which is simply 100 squares arranged in a ten-by-ten grid. Many schools use a 100-square learning carpet as a tool for active learning at all grade levels. This is a large floor carpet with 100 squares. Students physically place and move objects and number cards on the carpet. It is often used for concepts such as numeration, patterning, measurement, graphing and mapping skills.

Using a learning carpet at school or a 100-square chart at home gives visual and kinesthetic learners the benefit of seeing concepts demonstrated in a concrete way. It gives students an opportunity to gain confidence and practice with a concept before moving on to pencil and paper tasks. Using a 100-square chart with your child at home is a fun and easy way to practice and extend your child's math skills.

The Basics

Math is like a building and it needs to start with a good, solid foundation on which to build other math concepts. The foundation is what we call numeracy or simply "number." This branch of math includes numbers, number systems and their operations, and requires a specific, concrete type of thinking and a lot of memory work. Children need a lot of practice so that they can effortlessly and automatically add, subtract, multiply and divide in their heads. Practice is needed to achieve mastery.

Kids need an automatic command of the basic facts in order to prepare themselves to handle more challenging problems. If the child is stumbling over the basics, then problem solving and more advanced branches of math will be difficult. When a child has a good grasp of numbers and operations, it prepares her mind for higher-level math concepts like algebra, which requires an abstract way of thinking. Kids need to take small steps and learn the basics to lay a solid base on which to build other math skills. If your child is having difficulty, it may be that there has not been enough math drill and practice at school for your child. For the ideas to set in and be cemented, she may need additional practice at home. It is a good idea for all children, whether they are struggling or not, to review and practice basic math facts on a regular basis in order to stay sharp.

What Are the Basics?

- Know how to add, subtract, multiply and divide.
- Know addition and subtraction to 20.
- Know the times tables from 1 to 12 off by heart by the end of elementary school. (There is no need to memorize division tables since division is the inverse of multiplication.)
- Do simple adding, subtracting, multiplying and dividing in your head. This is called mental math.

Mental math is a valuable skill that enables us to make quick calculations. Even though we live in an era where we are surrounded by computers, cell phones, calculators and cash registers that can calculate for us, mental math is still a very much-needed skill. If your child doesn't know the times tables, she can't factor. If she can't factor, she can't do high school level strands of math, especially algebra. A high school tutor we know tells stories about high school students who aren't able to complete a math test or exam in the allotted time. They are spending too much time trying to figure out what 9 times 8 is, for example, when that basic calculation is just one small step in the whole question. Children who have memorized and mastered basic math facts have an advantage. It's much easier to learn the basics at a young age than to play catch up later.

There are fun ways to learn the basics, such as listening to songs on commercially made math CDs (these are available online or at educational supply stores), playing math drill games, playing computer games and using a blackboard or whiteboard to practice computation and problem solving.

The Four Operations

Operation (VERB)	Symbol	Solution	Example (how you say it)
Addition (ADD)	+	Sum	4 + 8 = 12 (4 plus 8 is 12)
Subtraction (SUBTRACT)	–	Difference	12 – 4 = 8 (12 minus 4 is 8)
Multiplication (MULTIPLY)	x	Product	4 X 8 = 32 (4 times 8 is 32)
Division (DIVIDE)	/ or ÷	Quotient	8 ÷ 4 = 2 (8 divided by 4 is 2)

Multiplication Times Tables

If your child feels overwhelmed by the task of learning the times tables, you can boost his confidence and help him along by sharing these tips we pass along to our students.

- The 0, 1, 10 and 11 times tables are easy as pie.
- The 2's are easy. You just double the number (or add it to itself) to get the answer.
- The 5's are easy. Every answer ends in either 0 or a 5.

X	1	2	3	4	5	6	7	8	9	10	11	12
1	1	2	3	4	5	6	7	8	9	10	11	12
2	2	4	6	8	10	12	14	16	18	20	22	24
3	3	6	9	12	15	18	21	24	27	30	33	36
4	4	8	12	16	20	24	28	32	36	40	44	48
5	5	10	15	20	25	30	35	40	45	50	55	60
6	6	12	18	24	30	36	42	48	54	60	66	72
7	7	14	21	28	35	42	49	56	63	70	77	84
8	8	16	24	32	40	48	56	64	72	80	88	96
9	9	18	27	36	45	54	63	72	81	90	99	108
10	10	20	30	40	50	60	70	80	90	100	110	120
11	11	22	33	44	55	66	77	88	99	110	121	132
12	12	24	36	48	60	72	84	96	108	120	132	144

- The 9's are easy. There is a pattern to them. When you add the digits of the answer together, they add up to 9. For example: 9 x 8 = 72 and 7 + 2 = 9.

Here is a way to use your hands to help with the 9 times table:

Hold up both hands in front of you with your palms facing you. Assign each finger a number, starting with your left thumb, which is number 1, and ending with your right thumb, which is number 10. If the question is 9 x 2, count to your second finger (it should be the index finger on your left hand), and curl that finger toward you. Now there is 1 finger up before the curled finger and 8 fingers up after the curled finger. So the answer is 18.

That leaves only the 3's, 4's, 6's, 7's 8's and 12's.

And remember, once you learn 6 x 7, for instance, you also know the answer to 7 x 6. That cuts down the memorization by half.

Math Curriculum

The elementary school math curriculum covers five strands, areas or standards. All strands involve problem solving. Each is covered in every grade so students continually build upon what they have already learned. The strands are as follows (we have used the US terminology, in Canada the names of the strands are slightly different):

Number and Operations

At home and in the community, numbers are everywhere. This strand investigates the four basic operations (addition, subtraction, multiplication and division). Other concepts covered include number systems, fractions, decimals, ratio, percent, factors and exponents, square roots, mental math, estimation, pencil and paper computation, learning to use a calculator, order of operations (in Canada, BEDMAS: brackets, exponents, division, multiplication, addition, subtraction; in the US, PEDMAS: parenthesis, exponents, division, multiplication, addition, subtraction).

Geometry

Understanding shapes and the spatial relationships of things around them helps children get ready for geometry. Other topics are points, lines, angles, figures, flips, slides, turns, grids and coordinates, 2-D and 3-D shapes.

Algebra

Patterns can be found in art, music, stories, nature and in numbers. They can be described in terms of repeating, growing, shrinking and other relationships as well as color, shape and size. Recognizing patterns and pattern rules helps children grasp the principles of algebra. In algebra, symbols (usually letters of the alphabet) represent numbers as in "$y + 7 = 18$."

Measurement

Money and time, height, width and length can be measured. Measurement is also used to determine the area, volume, space, capacity or amount an item takes up or holds. Units of measure are perimeter, area, capacity, volume and mass.

Data Analysis and Probability

Data analysis means collecting, organizing and interpreting information, sometimes using charts, tables and graphs. Probability is a measure of how likely it is that something will happen. Predicting and estimating are also covered in this strand.

Ways to Help Your Child with Math

Attitude

- Have a positive attitude about math.
- Stress that math is all about accuracy.
- If math is a weak area, accept this fact and have your child work extra hard to strengthen it.
- Expect some confusion and mistakes as part of the learning process. Be patient.
- Avoid negative comments such as "You'll never use this," or "I was no good in math."

Practice

- Provide lots of opportunities to do math as it makes her think and makes her brain work.
- Encourage your child to try solving a problem in different ways.
- If your child is struggling, go back to the basics and see if you can pinpoint where she got lost.
- Practice and drill addition and subtraction facts and multiplication times tables until they are mastered.

Calculators

When to Use a Calculator

It is imperative for children to know the basic facts, have the basic operations firmly implanted in their long-term memories and be able to do mental calculations before relying on a calculator. Children also need to develop their critical thinking and estimating skills; otherwise how will they know whether the answer they see displayed on a calculator is reasonable? Calculators are useful tools and suitable for complex operations, not basic math. It is fine to use a calculator for checking homework, doing quick calculations or playing number games for fun.

What Calculators Can't Do

When it comes to expanding and factoring, only our minds can do both operations. If a child is asked to factor 12, she should systematically and mentally go through her memory to recover 1 x 12 = 12 and 2 x 6 = 12 and 3 x 4 = 12 and so on; therefore, the factors of 12 are 1, 2, 3, 4, 6 and 12. A child who does not know basic multiplication (and division) facts will have a really hard time factoring. Knowing how to find the factors of a number will be very useful in high school when students must apply their factoring skills in algebra. Calculators cannot factor. Calculators can only expand, for example, 3 x 4 = 12.

Homework

- Try your best to help with homework, but remember, methods of teaching math have evolved and changed.
- Explain the math by following an example in the textbook.
- Refer to your child's notebook or textbook to familiarize yourself with math terminology.
- Show your child the way you learned the math when you were young, but if this is confusing your child, talk to the teacher for guidance.
- Work with your child until he has a solid grasp of the concept.

Routine

- Stay on top of the curriculum.
- Devote time each day to develop math proficiency.
- If your child has missed a math class, get her to ask the teacher to go over the lesson with her, as each math lesson builds on what has been previously taught.

Additional Help

- Get help early if required, as math is a progressive subject and it will get harder each year.
- Get an older sibling or friend to assist in teaching or going over the math. Children often respond better to someone other than you, the parent.
- If your child is having difficulty, contact the teacher to see if additional help during or after school is an option.
- Consider hiring a tutor.

Concrete Materials

- Use flashcards, a white board, etc. (whatever will help).
- Provide supplies such as pencil, ruler, eraser, compass, protractor, calculator, counters (such as dried beans), graph paper, building blocks, watch or clock, money (optional).

How to Solve a One-Step Problem

Here is a logical method we use with our students. You can follow it with your child at home. Even though there are a lot of steps to solving the problem, they soon become automatic.

Sample problem:

Julia and Amelia went to the beach on July 22. Before lunch, they collected 15 seashells. After lunch, they collected 23 seashells. How many seashells did they collect altogether?

1. Read the question. Read it again.
2. Close your eyes and picture what is going on.
3. Tell someone how you are going to solve the problem.
4. Draw a picture.
5. Circle any relevant numbers in the problem. Don't be tricked by the 22 in July 22.
6. Choose an operation. There are only four: addition, subtraction, multiplication and division. For this problem, the correct operation is addition.
7. Make a number sentence: $15 + 23 = 38$.
8. Solve the problem and show all your calculations. If required, write your answer in sentence form. For example, Julia and Amelia collected 38 seashells altogether.

9. Check to make sure your answer is correct.
10. Make sure you answered the question.

How to Solve a Multi-Step Problem

Here is a logical method to solve a multi-step problem that you can use with your child at home.

Sample problem:
There were 42 oranges in each crate on the truck from Florida. Twelve crates were delivered. When the crates were opened, 4 rotten oranges were found and discarded. The rest of the oranges were put into baskets of 10 oranges. How many baskets were needed?

Understanding the Problem
　1. What information am I given?
　2. What have I been asked to find?
　3. Restate the problem using your own words, or a sketch, table or list.

Making a Plan
　4. Do I know a related or similar problem? If yes, describe it.
　5. Do I need more information? If yes, describe.
　6. Consider different strategies such as finding a simple problem within the problem you are trying to solve, identify a pattern, use guess and check, decide which strand of mathematics will help you solve the problem (for example, operations, geometry, algebra, probability).

Carrying out the Plan
　7. Do the calculations.
　　　$42 \times 12 = 504$
　　　$504 - 4 = 500$
　　　$500 \div 10 = 50$
　　　There were 50 baskets needed.

Looking Back at the Solution
　8. Is my answer reasonable? If no, then go back to Step 3.
　9. Are my units correct? If no, then go back to Step 3.
　10. Can I use a different strategy? If yes, which one?
　11. Is the strategy used effective? If yes or no, explain why.

Math in High School and Beyond

It's hard to tell in elementary school what math courses your child might want or need to take in high school or beyond, so it is important to place an emphasis on math and to keep her skills strong in all strands of math. Once your child is in high school, it will be difficult for her to follow math lessons if she has not fully understood the concepts taught in elementary school. Some kids get satisfactory marks in math in elementary school, but when they reach high school, areas of weakness become magnified once the math gets more complex.

Math is all around us and plays an important part in our everyday lives. The curriculum in elementary and high school demands math. Certain careers have math prerequisites. Math is needed in any job that requires higher education such as as engineer, doctor, dentist, pharmacist, nurse, middle and high school teacher, accountant, financial planner and drafter. Good math skills are required to pass a General Education Development (GED) test or a Scholastic Aptitude Test (SAT).

By strengthening your child's math skills at home, you are helping her become an independent thinker and establishing the foundations for lifelong numeracy.

- Make math a part of every day life in your home
- Start young and use concrete materials
- Help your child learn and master the basics
- Know the curriculum
- Help your child with math at home especially if she is having difficulty
- Review the steps to problem solving with your child

Chapter 8

Homework and Study Skills

After the teacher has done his or her bit for the day, it is your turn to take over. Your child has been returned to you and it's now up to you to continue the teaching. Don't worry, it's not formal teaching. It's overseeing the homework, chatting, listening, enjoying, reminding, helping, editing, coaching and guiding. Learning does not stop when your child leaves the classroom. There is no such thing as "you are done learning for the day."

Homework should not be a bad word. Don't make homework the enemy. In your home, it should be expected that homework will be completed and done well. Remember, your child will be in school for many more years, so it's a good idea to make homework a routine part of daily life at home very early on.

Our philosophy is "homework comes first" and extracurricular activities come second. By "homework comes first," we mean that its importance is valued, it is a priority, a given and it will be done. "Vegging" out, snacking, hanging out with friends, taking lessons, participating in sports and taking part in other activities or clubs are all important to a child's growth and development. Be flexible, be creative and learn to juggle all of these interests or pursuits around homework.

Homework generally falls into one of four categories: daily debriefing, unfinished classroom work, an assignment or practice.

Daily Debriefing

By this we mean an informal chat about your child's day at school. It's all in the questioning. Go beyond: "How was school today?" Try asking: "What is one new thing you learned today?" or "What was the best part of your day?" or "Did you leave the classroom today for library, gym, an assembly, etc.?" or "What were you working on in Science today?" or "What did the teacher read to you today?" Questions and answers do not have to pertain to academic subjects only, but any aspect of school life. This daily banter is a wonderful way to connect with your child and to make connections between classroom learning and personal experiences.

For example, if your child is learning about the Great Lakes, you might remind him about the family visit to Niagara Falls, pointing out that the falls empty into Lake Ontario from Lake Erie. This is also a golden opportunity to teach the acronym and memory aid HOMES, which stands for the names of the Great Lakes—Huron, Ontario, Michigan, Erie and Superior.

Another example might be if your child is studying all about plants and seeds. To extend this learning experience, take two apples, cut one in half horizontally and one vertically. Notice and talk about the patterns that are formed in each apple half. Take the seeds out. Count them. Plant them. Make applesauce. Read a book about Johnny Appleseed. Eat cut-up apples for dessert. Use your own experience and imagination to come up with more ways to continue the apple theme and have fun while learning. Teach your child that knowledge is everywhere, and help him to make connections between what he has learned at school and the big world around him.

Unfinished Classroom Work

Sometimes a child does not complete his work in the class time allotted. For example, the teacher has provided ample class time to complete 10 math questions. Your child has only finished seven. The remaining three questions will probably be assigned for homework. Homework completion is documented by the teacher.

An Assignment

This could be making a model or a diorama, writing a newspaper article, essay or speech, preparing a research assignment or skit. A good teacher provides students (and, in turn, their parents) with a guideline, or worksheet, which will include the following:

- topic
- what has to be covered
- type of presentation—essay, Bristol board display, diorama, speech, etc.
- timeline
- due date
- a marking scheme or rubric (see page 102 for a sample rubric)
- how the assignment will be done—alone, in pairs or in a group
- where the work will take place—at home or at school or a combination of both places
- parental signature

See page 104 for a step-by-step guide to doing a research project, which is a large assignment usually given with more time.

Practice

This type of homework is perpetual and can be done without a reminder from the teacher. For example: reading or studying, practicing printing or handwriting, drilling times tables, reviewing adding and subtracting facts, studying formulas or memorizing a speech or a poem.

If your child is fuzzy about what homework he has, remind him that it is his responsibility to know. Encourage him to listen carefully when the teacher assigns homework, and to write it down in his school agenda or notebook. If the problem persists, make an appointment to see the teacher with your child (and his agenda) in attendance.

Homework FAQs

Why is homework important?
It is important for everyone, including children, to finish what they start. Completing work at home ties up loose ends, reinforces skills, cements concepts and allows the child to savor a sense of accomplishment. Homework is also practice. To master any skill, practice is essential. Think of learning how to play a musical instrument. If you were studying piano, you would not make any progress if you just attended a weekly lesson and did nothing in between. Practice, practice, practice.

How do I know if my child has homework?
Start by asking your child if he has any homework. In many schools an agenda or planner is provided for students to jot down their homework. Some schools even require a teacher and parent signature each day, to make sure that everybody is up to date. Some teachers send newsletters or notes home outlining upcoming class studies, assignments and due dates. Most schools have a website and some schools have a system where each teacher posts class information. If you still have questions about homework, contact the teacher.

Why is it important for my child to finish homework on time?
Assigned homework is usually collected or taken up the next day. Homework reinforces the concepts that were taught throughout

the day and lays the groundwork for the next lesson. Homework completion is usually part of the overall report card mark. Finishing homework establishes good organizational skills and routines.

How much homework is to be expected of my child?
Homework policies and procedures vary depending on the school and school district. Check the guidelines for your school. Even if homework has not been assigned, you should continue to talk to your child about what he is learning, keep reading together, and encourage him to practice and study. Just to give you a rough idea, the school board where we taught suggested no homework be assigned in kindergarten; approximately 20 minutes of homework for grades 1 to 3; approximately 40 minutes for grades 4 to 6; approximately 60 minutes for grades 7 and 8. Some nights there will be no homework, and other nights there may be more than the suggested amount.

How much homework help should I give?
It is your job to oversee the homework and it is your child's job and responsibility to do the work. You can help by reminding, guiding, walking through the steps and, perhaps, following an example from the textbook or notebook. If your child is having difficulty grasping a concept, try explaining it in your own words. Sometimes, hearing a different person's explanation can "make the light go on." However, if you help your child too much, if you do the work, if you correct every single mistake and change the essence of your child's work, you have gone too far. When the teacher looks at homework, it should look very similar to the work the child produces in the classroom each day. A parent was once overheard saying, "I just can't believe that my son only got 63% on his science fair project. I worked so hard and I thought I did such a good job."

Where do I get extra help for my child?
If your child is having difficulty in a certain academic area try to help your child out yourself, enlist the help of a sibling, an older student or another adult, contact the teacher for additional help or look for a homework support program through the school, community or the public library. There are many private companies and individuals outside the school that offering tutoring. It is a personal decision whether or not to hire a tutor.

No homework?

There have been articles written recently about parents opting out of homework for their children. Some parents feel that there is too much homework and it takes away from family time and extracurricular activities. They want their children to be evaluated solely on in-class work. Some schools are adopting a no-homework policy.

Homework and Study Essentials

Special place in the home (with a table, a chair, good lighting and ample workspace). Many kids start out using the kitchen or dining room table as a homework spot so that parents can keep an eye on what's going on (and make dinner at the same time). As they get older, many kids end up doing homework at a desk in their bedroom.

Basic supplies (such as pencil, paper, highlighters, colored pencils, markers, ruler, eraser, scissors, tape, glue, white-out, calculator, Post-it notes, paper—both lined and unlined). Teachers often hear "I don't have a _____ at home." Sometimes it is true, sometimes it is not. If your home is not equipped, you can buy supplies inexpensively at a dollar store.

Handy reference materials (desktop alphabet, times table chart, dictionary, thesaurus, atlas, almanac and a globe). Some families prefer to have these reference materials in book form while other families rely on the computer for reference help.

It's a good idea to bookmark both the school and public library web pages. Bookmark the library catalogue, the database pages and kids or teen homework help pages. Here are some other valuable websites:

- **Google** (www.google.com): To find a definition for a word or phrase, go to Google, type the word "define" followed by a space, then the word you want to define. To see definitions from several sources, type "define" followed by a colon, then the word or phrase. For example, define: rock

- **Dictionary** (www.dictionary.com): This website also has a thesaurus, encyclopedia, translator and web definitions.

- **Thesaurus** (www.thesaurus.com)

- **Quotations** (www.bartleby.com/quotations)

- **Bibliography** (www.easybib.com)

- **Encyclopedia** (www.encyclopedia.com) or (www.wikipedia.com): When doing research on Wikipedia, students should not just read the main article, but use the references at the bottom to link to original sources.

How do I make homework a positive experience for my child?
After school but before homework, let your child unwind, relax and
have a snack. A little physical activity will help your child expend
some energy, reenergize and focus on the work at hand. Build in
a break, check in and see how things are progressing, give help if
needed, encourage your child and give the work a quick once-over
when it is finished.

An organized backpack. It is definitely the responsibility of the child to pack
and unpack the schoolbag, but you will probably need to supervise the
operation to avoid the horrors of moldy sandwiches and obsolete newsletters
in the bottom of the bag. Younger children will need reminding that it is
library day, gym day, pizza day, etc. Older children should be self-sufficient.

The homework assignment, notebook, notes and textbook brought home
from school.

Test material and format. Know what is expected, what the test will be
based on and the test format.

A computer with Internet access in your home or at a library. The computer
is a good tool for locating information for a research project, for note taking,
for writing the final copy of a research assignment, for using the dictionary,
thesaurus and atlas features. However, a computer is not always needed
to complete the daily homework. If your child insists he needs to use the
computer to complete homework, ask: "What exactly do you need it for?"
See page 160 for tips on Internet safety.

Quiet, distraction-free atmosphere. Your child needs an environment that
is conducive to concentration. TVs, phones and computers should either
be turned off or not in the homework area at all. The right frame of mind is
focused and ready to study.

A routine or schedule. The same time set aside every day is ideal, but may
not be possible. Be flexible. Get a good night's sleep before the big test.

A timeline. Budget homework time and don't leave printing an assignment
to the last minute because, as "Murphy's Law" dictates, if something can
go wrong, it will go wrong and your printer will break down or run out of ink.
Guaranteed.

There will inevitably be times when your child is unable to finish the homework assignment. It may be that your child is not feeling well, is overtired, is upset about something, is frustrated with the homework or there is just too much work for one evening. Or the dog ate it! Be kind, be flexible, excuse the homework for once and drop the teacher a note explaining the situation. A parent we know once sent in a note that read: "Please excuse my son for not completing his homework as he was over tired and under motivated."

What do I do if homework is a battle?
Ideally, homework should never get to the war-zone stage. If good homework habits are firmly entrenched at an early age, it is less likely that a battle will ensue.

If homework has already become an issue, you need a fresh start. Call a family meeting and brainstorm ideas and possible solutions. Explain your frustrations and let your child do the same. Set some new ground rules, but the bottom line is, homework must be finished and it must be done well. Give praise when the homework is completed, offer an incentive when your child gets down to work without complaining or arguing, and celebrate when you see a new and more positive pattern starting to emerge.

When do I stop helping with homework?
As your child gets older and the routine of doing homework is well established, your role primarily becomes one of overseer, editor and coach. If your child is experiencing difficulties grasping a concept, you may need to spend more time explaining and helping.

What if I can't help because I don't understand the work?
As the parent, you should always be on top of things but you may not have all the answers. If you studied in a different language, did not study a certain subject, did poorly in a certain subject or have forgotten what you learned, don't give up. Get your child extra help if he needs it.

Study Methods

There is a big difference between a spelling test for a six-year-old and a history test for a thirteen-year-old. A young child has to be walked through the studying process, be taught study skills and be quizzed after he studies.

How to Help a Young Child Prepare for a Test

Here are some tips for helping a young child prepare for a test:
- Sit with your child and guide him through the process. It will be necessary to work together a number of times before your child is able to study effectively on his own. Even when your child is able to review the materials independently, you should still check in frequently and quiz him when he has finished studying.
- Have your child read over the materials that he has brought home, for example, textbook, notebook, booklet.
- Ask your child to tell you what he knows about the topic.
- Ask your child questions based on the information in the materials.
- Ask him if there is anything he does not understand.
- Repeat for any areas of difficulty.

How to Study for a Spelling Test

Here are six steps that you can review with your child of any age to study for a spelling test:
- Look at the word.
- Say the word out loud.
- Cover the word.
- Spell the word out loud or write it down.
- Check to see if the answer was correct.
- Repeat the process for any word that was not correct.

Three Study Methods for Middle and Upper Grade Students

Here are three study methods that are most widely used by middle and upper grade students. You can give these instructions to your child.

The In-Your-Head Method

Read: Read a small section of material either from your notes or the textbook. Focus on key words, headings, boldface print, anything in italics, captions, etc. Read it over more than once.

Look Away

Recite: Tell yourself out loud or in your head what you have just read.

Check: Look back at the material to see if you remembered everything. If you have remembered everything in this section move on to the next. Take a short break between sections. When you have finished studying everything, have somebody quiz you if possible.

The Pencil-to-Paper Method

Read and Write: As you read each section of material, make point form notes of the main ideas. Focus on key words, headings, boldface print, anything in italics, captions, etc.

Review: Read over your point form notes.

Check: Cover up your notes and see if you can recite them out loud or in your head. If you have remembered everything in this section move on to the next. Take a short break between sections. When you have finished studying everything, have somebody quiz you if possible.

A word of caution about studying with a friend: Although children start out with good intentions (buddy study) it doesn't take much for them to get off topic and be distracted. One session might be helpful, but most studying should be done individually.

Individualized Method

You and your child will have to determine what study method works best for him. It could be that you modify the above approaches or that you add study aids such as diagrams, charts or other types of graphic organizers, a tape recorder, homemade memory aids or whatever works to help your child remember the necessary information.

Memory Aids

One device used to help remember information is an acronym, which is an abbreviation made up of the first letter or first part of a word designed to help jog the memory when studying: One such acronym is ROY G. BIV, which refers to the colors of the spectrum in order— red, orange, yellow, green, blue, indigo and violet

Encourage your child to use any trick, acronym or short form, either existing or made up, that will help him remember.

Tips on How to Quiz Your Child

Only when your child has finished studying everything do you step in and test his knowledge. When quizzing your child, be sure he understands the concept and hasn't just memorized a bunch of words.

Try turning the chapter headings into questions. Give him a key word or phrase and ask him to explain and elaborate. Sometimes there are questions already provided at the end of each chapter in the textbook or the teacher has given a study guide that you could refer to.

How to Write a Test

Here are some tips on how to write a test. You should go over them with your child.

- As soon as you receive the test paper, do not read it but rather turn it over and quickly jot down any acronyms, formulas, dates or other important facts that you don't want to forget. This will take away the stress of having to remember them later while completing your answers.
- Turn the test paper back over and quickly read over every question.
- Start by answering the questions that you are really sure you know the answer to. Nobody ever said that you have to start with the first question and continue on in order.
- If the test has different types of questions, start with the kind you are best at, for example, fill in the blanks.
- Next, go back and answer the questions that are worth the most marks.
- Pace yourself.
- Before answering an essay question, underline key words in the question. Flip the paper over or use a margin to jot down a rough outline for your answer. You should have an introduction, body and conclusion.
- Answer any remaining questions.
- Read over all your answers. Correct any mistakes.
- Don't leave any questions unanswered. Make an educated guess. Any answer is better than no answer.
- If there is still time, go back to an essay question and add more facts to the body of your answer. Be careful not to say the same thing over and over.
- When reviewing your answers, don't second-guess yourself. The first answer that pops into your head is often the right one.
- For math tests, show your rough work.
- Double-check your math calculations and ask yourself if your answer makes sense.

What Is a Rubric?

A common method of marking is a rubric. A rubric is an evaluation tool that lists criteria for an assignment. It describes the level of quality for each criterion. The rubric is often given out with the assignment to clarify the teacher's expectations. When the rubric is filled in by the teacher, it clearly shows the student (and parents) why the child got the grade he did. It also shows what the child can do to improve.

Criteria	Sources	Punctuation, Grammar and Spelling	Organization	Content Knowledge
1	Only one source was used.	There are a number of major errors in punctuation, grammar and spelling making it difficult to read.	Information is disorganized and there are gaps in content.	Student demonstrates limited understanding of the subject.
2	One or two sources were used.	There are a few major errors in punctuation, grammar and spelling.	Information is somewhat organized. Paragraphs do not flow well.	Student demonstrates some understanding of the subject.
3	Three or four sources were used.	There are a few minor errors in punctuation, grammar and spelling.	Information is organized in well-constructed paragraphs and flows well.	Student demonstrates considerable understanding of the subject.
4	More than four sources were used.	There are no punctuation, grammar or spelling errors.	Information is very organized in well-constructed paragraphs that follow a logical sequence.	Student demonstrates a thorough understanding of the subject.
Mark				

Teacher Comments:

Basic Writing Skills

Some very important skills for a child to master that will help him throughout his years in school are writing a sentence, paragraph, essay and how to do a research project.

How to Write a Sentence

A sentence starts with a capital letter and ends with a period, a question mark or an exclamation mark. It has a **subject** (a person, place or thing) and a *verb* (an action word). It expresses a complete thought. For example:

Young **Morgan** *drank* his milk.

How to Write a Paragraph

A paragraph is made up of a number of sentences. The first sentence answers a question or gives an opinion on a topic. The following sentences support the first sentence. The last sentence is a concluding sentence that rephrases the first sentence. For example:

I love my father very much. He lets me help him vacuum. He teaches me many things like how to use a screwdriver. Every night we share a bedtime story. My dad is the best dad in the whole wide world.

How to Write an Essay

This is an outline describing how to write an essay. You can go over it with your child.

Introductory Paragraph: The introduction should start with a good opening line or quote or anecdote that pertains to the topic. It should end with a thesis. The thesis is the focus or main idea of the essay.

The Body of the Essay in Paragraphs: Start each paragraph with a topic sentence restating a main idea. Cite evidence or give examples to support this first sentence. These points are the main ideas of the paragraph.

Concluding Paragraph: The conclusion is a wrap-up of the essay. Ask yourself: "Did I prove everything I said I was going to?"

An essay should be a polished piece of prose, well written in your own words, free of grammar, spelling and typing mistakes. An essay should sound like you; it should not sound the work of a university professor. It should be organized and tidy.

Example of a Five-Paragraph Essay

The title and thesis statement are in bold. Topic sentences are in italics. Main ideas of each paragraph are underlined.

Dogs

Lots of families enjoy dogs as pets. Dogs come in many shapes and sizes. They need people to feed and take care of them. Dogs can do lots of fun things.

There are a lot of different kinds of dogs. <u>Some are big and fluffy and some are small and sweet.</u> There are dogs that are small enough to fit in a purse and dogs that look like small horses. Some dogs even look like their owners.

Even though having a dog is great, you still have to take care of them. <u>Dogs need exercise, so you have to walk them every day. A dog also needs to eat every day just like we do.</u> You can't forget to feed them or they will get sick.

There are a lot of fun things you can do with a dog. <u>You can run with your dog and play catch. You can pet them and teach them tricks. The best thing about dogs is that they are your best friend.</u> No matter what happens you can always count on a dog to make you feel better.

A dog is a great thing to add to the family. Everybody will love and enjoy it.

Research Projects

Inevitably the day will arrive when your child comes home and says, "I have to do a project on dogs." Why are research projects assigned?

- To develop library, research and organizational skills
- To provide an opportunity to develop informational writing skills
- To consolidate skills and ideas taught in class
- To prepare for tests
- To further investigate a topic touched on in class

Here is a step-by-step guide to doing a research project. You can go over the steps with your child.

Step 1: Preparation

- **Select a topic.**
- **Choose materials.** The teacher will indicate the number of sources required. Keep an ongoing list of resources used for a bibliography. These sources should vary, for example, books, encyclopedias, magazines, pamphlets, DVDs, Internet and interviews. Look up books from home by accessing the public library catalog.

Step 2: Organization

- **Headings or thesis.** Younger students are usually asked to brainstorm and prepare a web of ideas or headings. Sometimes the teacher supplies the headings. Older students may be required to write a thesis. Thesis statements articulate the intent of your paper and express a clear opinion or answer a research question.
- **Make an outline.** Here is an example of an outline:

> DOGS
> Introduction
> Body
> > Appearance
> > Behavior
> > Habitat
> > Diet
> > Enemies
> > Adaptations
> > Classifications
> > Life Cycle/Reproduction
> Any extras (maps, diagrams, pictures)
> Conclusion
> Bibliography

Step 3: Drafts

- **Make point form notes.** There are two methods: see Method A and Method B below. Start reading for information. Read a chapter or section at a time. Pay attention to chapter headings, subheadings, captions and the first and last sentence of each paragraph and summary paragraphs to get the general ideas.

Go back and read carefully for key points. Then write down key information, the main idea or just enough words to make sense. Use your own words. Do not copy whole sentences word for word. These notes are not sentences. They do not start with a capital letter or end with a period. Start with a dash or bullet. Every new point goes on a new line. Even though these notes are called "rough," they should be tidy and accurate.

There are two basic methods to organize point form notes.

Method A: Write down one heading or main idea on the top of each page. Make careful point form notes under the appropriate headings. Here is an example of what this might look like for the topic "Dogs":

Enemies
- man
- in some countries dog meat is eaten
- other animals such as monkeys and wolves can attack and kill

Method B: Make notes as you read. List all point form notes under one heading, for example, "Dogs." The next step is to sort your notes by highlighting with different colored highlighters, number or letter coding, cutting and pasting or copying them under the appropriate heading. Here is an example of a point form list under one heading:

Dogs
- man can be a dog's enemy
- commercial dog food can be wet or dry
- 5,000 breeds of dogs
- "dog is man's best friend"
- need to hire a dog sitter while away
- requires money, grooming, training, exercise

- **Write the draft.** Put your point form notes into sentences that sound like you. Write the body of your research project in paragraphs. Make sure your work makes sense, is in a logical order and provides enough information. Write an introduction. Write a conclusion. Refer back to "How to Write an Essay."

- **Proofread and edit your draft.** Have someone else go over this rough copy.

Step 4: Final Product

- **Write the good copy.** Make sure your final, polished good copy looks neat, is well-organized and free from errors and typos. Include any extras or finishing touches like a map, a picture, a chart, a drawing, a fancy title page, table of contents and a cover. Impress the teacher, dazzle her, put her in a good mood and make her want to read your work.

Bibliography

A bibliography is a list of all the resources you used to gather information. Each time you use a resource, record all the information needed to complete a bibliography. Check with the classroom teacher for an example of the bibliographic format required, as the formats vary. There are online bibliography makers such www.easybib.com where you enter the information and a bibliography is generated. Bibliographies are sometimes called "Works Cited."

How to Write a Bibliography

- Follow the format the teacher has given.
- List sources in alphabetical order by author's last name.
- Sources that do not have authors are alphabetized by title.
- Numbers are not used when listing the sources.
- After the first line of an entry, indent each additional line.
- Titles are italicized if typed and underlined if handwritten.
- Make sure to include online sources, including magazines and encyclopedias.

Academic Honesty

Academic honesty means giving credit where credit is due when writing a research paper and using the ideas of others. Be careful not to plagiarize. Plagiarism means to use or copy someone else's ideas, word for word, and pass them off as your own without giving credit to the author. Plagiarism is considered cheating.

Homework, research projects and study skills should become routine and well established to be effective.

- Supply the essentials for homework and studying
- Remember that it is up to your child to know the homework assignment and to do the work
- Parents should give assistance and encouragement
- Help your child discover the study method that works best for him
- Quiz your kid after he studies
- Be sure your child knows the proper format when writing a sentence, paragraph, essay, research project or bibliography

Chapter 9

Respect, Behavior and Discipline

We are subject to rules in every aspect of our lives. Rules are designed to keep everyone safe, to govern conduct and maintain order. At school there is a code of conduct that outlines rules and regulations that all students are expected to follow. Believe it or not, we have actually heard these words from parents: "These are great school rules and I support them wholeheartedly, but in this case, can't you see, they just don't apply to my child." The rules should, and do, apply to all children. Parents and teachers are trying to prepare children for life in "the big world" after their schooling is finished, and in the big world, rules apply to everyone. The red light means stop for all. The fact that school rules apply to everyone makes every student equal and provides a level playing field for all.

School Code of Conduct

The school's code of conduct provides guiding principles for student behavior. The rules are provided to families in written form on the school website, in booklets, in student agendas and in school newsletters. They are addressed and reviewed at school in assemblies, in classroom lessons and, sometimes, through daily announcements. The code of conduct addresses the following areas:
- **Respect** (for self, others, property and authority)
- **Responsibility** (each student is responsible for his own behavior)
- **Safety** (on the bus, in the yard, halls, classrooms, washroom)
- **Bullying** (outlines expectations and steps for students to follow)
- **Technology** (safe computer/Internet use),
- **Banned items** (alcohol, tobacco, drugs, weapons),
- **Personal electronic devices** (cell phones, iPods, mp3 players)
- **Dress code** (uniform requirements or list of acceptable clothing)

Schools seek to create a positive climate for the safety and well-being of all students. Students take part in character building and anti-bullying programs. Some schools have peer mediation programs. Older children are trained to help younger children find peaceful resolutions to situations in the schoolyard. At the same time, they are teaching problem solving skills.

Consequences

The code of conduct also gives information about the consequences for inappropriate behavior. Consequences vary according to the severity of the misbehavior. For minor incidents, the consequence may be as simple as the teacher speaking with the student, pointing out the problem and helping the student make a plan for how to do better next time. For more serious incidents, consequences can include loss of privileges or a detention, and in extreme cases, suspension or expulsion.

In the Classroom

The expectation in the class is that the children will be well behaved. A good teacher sets the tone for good behavior in the classroom by being consistent and following through. Kids like to know their boundaries and know exactly what will happen to them if them step out of bounds.

At the beginning of the school year, many teachers work with students to make up the class rules. Most children know what makes for a comfortable, safe environment that is conducive to learning, and they rarely make suggestions that make the teacher's eyes roll back in her head. When students and teachers work together to establish ground rules, the children feel a sense of ownership and are less likely to disregard the rules.

The rules are usually stated in positive terms (for example, "Listen carefully to others" instead of "Don't interrupt") and are prominently displayed in the classroom. Consequences are clearly outlined. Common class rules or expectations could include any or all of the following:

- Be on time for class.
- Come to class prepared to work with all supplies.
- Pay attention, listen to instructions and follow them carefully.
- Raise your hand and wait to be called on before speaking.
- Participate in class discussions.
- Use your best manners.
- Show respect for self, teacher, classmates and property.
- Do nothing to keep the teacher from teaching and the others from learning.
- Give your best effort.
- Be cooperative.
- Do homework and complete all assignments neatly and on time.

Classroom teachers also have specific procedures for such things as classroom entry and dismissal, using the washroom, eating lunch, turning in work and sharpening pencils.

Teachers usually like to solve classroom issues within the confines of their own room. The last resort is to send the child to the office to be dealt with.

Teachers notice and acknowledge the positive behavior of their students. Positive consequences can include:

- a smile, a nod or a thumbs up
- verbal praise
- written praise
- good news note or phone call home
- a little reward (book mark, sticker, special pencil)
- a whole class treat (having independent reading time outside under a tree)
- trip to the principal's office to share a great test mark, a piece of art or sing a song

Classroom consequences for negative behavior could include any of the following:

- a look, a glance or a frown from the teacher (the "evil eye")
- private student-teacher discussion
- the "three strikes and you're out" approach. (Children are given two reminders for inappropriate behavior. The third time, action is taken.)
- "I" messages. (Instead of a teacher saying, "Stop yelling!" to a child, she says, "I want you to calm down and I need you to speak in a nicer way.")
- detention or loss of recess
- note to parents
- change of seats
- phone call home. (Our favorite principal always allowed the child to pick the parent she wanted to speak to. Then the principal would say, "Start dialing, start talking and hand the phone to me when you have told your mom or dad exactly what you did.")
- behavior contract. (Sometimes called a reflection paper, to be filled out by the child, explaining what he has done and making a plan for how to do better next time. This paper usually needs to be signed by a parent and returned to the school.)
- loss of a privilege
- confiscation of a "forbidden" item
- trip to the principal's office

Respect between Teachers and Students

The teachers we know who have the most wonderful rapport with their students all have one thing in common—they respect their students and their students respect them back. In this give-and-take relationship, there is a sense of trust and a feeling of caring. There is honest and open communication. If the student knows that the teacher has a genuine interest in her both academically and personally, she will be motivated to work hard and shine in that teacher's eyes.

Moving from Discipline to Self-Discipline

The "big picture" goal of rules and consequences is not to punish and impose discipline, but to help children move toward self-discipline. This is a process that takes time, a lot of support and ongoing encouragement to develop. Children will make mistakes along the way, but they will learn from the mistakes and keep moving ahead and forging on. When teachers and parents set reasonable limits for children and are consistent in following them through, they are providing a framework within which children will develop their sense of right and wrong. The aim is for children to start to think before they act. This is the beginning of self-control. In time, they start to follow rules not to please someone or to avoid punishment, but because they understand that it is the right thing to do.

Children with self-discipline demonstrate responsibility and ownership for their actions. They are more likely to do well at school and are justifiably proud of their accomplishments.

What Parents Can Do

Any strategies used in the classroom to develop good behavior, self-discipline and respect can be adapted and used at home. Children know what to expect at school, so do the same by teaching your children and making it very clear what you expect of them at home. It is important that parents:

- Support the decisions of the school.
- Talk in private to the teacher and not in front of your child if you are not in agreement with the teacher.

- Set up house rules and explain why they are important.
- Have consequences in place and be consistent in applying them.
- Make sure to follow through when you say you are going to do something.
- Avoid bailing your child out and making excuses for poor behavior. (Children need to face the consequences of their actions and learn from their mistakes.)
- Be flexible when flexibility and compassion are called for.
- Adjust rules and consequences as your child gets older and becomes more responsible.
- Work on developing and maintaining mutual respect between you and your child.

Rules at school and at home are designed to keep children safe and to keep things running smoothly.

- Schools have a code of conduct that students are expected to follow
- Classroom teachers have guidelines that are sometimes made in conjunction with the students
- Consequences for breaking rules are designed to help children learn from their mistakes
- When adults treat children with respect, children are likely to reciprocate
- The goal of discipline is to help develop self-discipline in children
- Classroom strategies can be adapted and used effectively at home

Chapter 10
Special Education

Special Education provides specially designed, individualized instruction for students with special needs. Special needs students (also called exceptional students) run the gamut from those who need only small adjustments in the classroom to those who have multiple disabilities and require extensive support and intervention. Intellectually gifted students also fall under the umbrella of Special Education. The goal of Special Education is to promote student success by providing services, equipment, curriculum and styles of teaching that are tailored to the unique needs of the child.

In the United States, Special Education is governed by the Individuals with Disabilities Education Act (IDEA). The IDEA states that all students are entitled to a free and appropriate public

Understanding the Terminology Used in Special Education

Accommodations, modifications and alternative programs are all terms that refer to changes a teacher makes to the way the curriculum is delivered or to the curriculum itself. They are usually outlined in an IEP.

Accommodations are small adjustments in teaching that a teacher makes to help a child be successful. The child is still working on grade level expectations.

Common accommodations (sometimes called strategies or adaptations) are:

- Using strategic seating to ensure the student's attention, for example, placing an easily distracted child at the front of the room so he can focus on his work and not the children all around him
- Giving additional time for a test or assignment
- Providing the child with clear, concise directions and having the child repeat back what he has heard
- Monitoring the child frequently to ensure she is on task
- Discussing and planning assignments in advance and checking in while work is being completed
- Providing visual aids
- Allowing the child to write tests in a quiet room
- Using technology, for example, voice-activated computer

education in the least restrictive environment. In Canada, each province has policies and procedures governing Special Education.

This chapter serves as a brief, basic overview of:

- the classifications/categories of special needs and a short definition for each
- the general process for identifying and programming for special needs children
- tips for parents who are making their way through the system

Those seeking more in-depth information should consult with teachers or Special Education staff at school or contact an association specializing in a specific special need.

- Reducing written output (quantity of work)
- Providing modified test methods, for example, oral versus written
- Scribing (writing what the student dictates) assignments or tests for a student

Good teachers use accommodations to ensure success not just for special needs students, but for all students.

Modifications are changes to the level of curriculum expectations. The expectations meet the learning needs of the child. They provide the student with goals that are achievable.

Common modifications are:

- Using expectations from a different grade level
- Reducing the number of expectations covered
- Reducing the amount of information to be learned
- Adapting goals to suit the needs of the learner

A small number of students require **alternative programs,** which are not from a grade-level curriculum, but focus on communication skills, self-help skills, social skill development and other skills appropriate to the individual needs of the student.

An **IEP (Individual Education Plan or Program)** is a written document that states the classification of the special need, outlines the child's strengths and areas of need, lays out learning goals and expectations, lists services and supports the child receives, and describes accommodations or modifications and lists assessment strategies.

Classifications for Special Needs

To receive special needs services, a student is usually formally identified as having one of these specific special needs. The process is the same whether the student has a mild or a severe need.

Although school districts may have slight differences in terminology, the basic classifications for special needs are as follows:

- **Autism/Pervasive Developmental Disorder:** a neurological disorder that causes developmental, social and communication problems. It can also include repetitive or restricted behavior. It affects the way the person interacts with the world. Autism, Asperger's Syndrome, Pervasive Developmental Disorder and Rett Syndrome are some autism spectrum disorders. Each person with an autism spectrum disorder develops differently.
- **Blind/Low Vision:** visual impairment or medically identified as blind
- **Deaf/Hearing Impairment:** hearing loss that ranges from mild to profound
- **Developmental Disability:** a physical or mental disability such as cerebral palsy, Down Syndrome or other genetic disorders
- **Emotional/Behavioral:** includes challenges such as Oppositional Defiant Disorder, Conduct Disorder, Obsessive Compulsive Disorder, Bipolar Disorder, Anxiety Disorder and Severe Depression
- **Gifted:** unusually advanced general intellectual ability that requires specialized learning experiences
- **Intellectual Disability:** significantly subaverage intellectual ability that affects development, learning and social functioning
- **Learning Disability:** a disorder that affects the way a person understands, remembers, expresses and processes information. It is the most prevalent of the special needs. Learning disabilities can range from mild to severe. Specialized strategies are taught and applied to help the student learn. Learning disabilities include:
  Attention Deficit Disorder and Attention Deficit Hyperactivity Disorder (ADD and ADHD): difficulty with attention span and impulse control, sometimes includes hyperactivity

Auditory Processing: how information is understood, difficulty with memory or accuracy of what is heard and/or difficulty comprehending multiple tasks

Dyscalculia: affects math skills

Dysgraphia: affects writing abilities. Could be a problem with spelling, poor handwriting or writing thoughts on paper

Dyspraxia (sensory integration disorder): a problem with motor skills, for example, hand-eye coordination, balance

Dyslexia: affects language and reading. Problems with phonological awareness (see Chapter 4)

Language Disorder: problems with verbal language skills and fluency

Memory: problems with long-term, short-term, working memory

Nonverbal: difficulty in social and physical areas, not related to language

Organizational: a time management and organizational disability

Reading: difficulty understanding text, difficulty with reading fluency and phonological awareness skills

Multiple Disabilities: a combination of the listed disabilities

Physical Disability: limits a person's ability to perform everyday tasks

Speech and Language Disability: a communication disorder that affects receptive and/or expressive language

Gifted students generally have a high level of verbal ability, are able to process information effectively and have flexibility of thinking. They are able to think abstractly, sense consequences and make generalizations. Most gifted students have a variety of interests and an advanced thought process. Identification of gifted students is usually based on academic performance, psychological assessment, teacher and parent input.

Programming for gifted students is based on grade-appropriate curriculum that is individualized to meet the needs of the student. Curriculum compacting is often used. This allows students to skip parts of the curriculum they have mastered and move on to extension activities. There is also a focus on critical thinking skills and refining social skills. The criteria for identification as a gifted student varies by state and province.

Steps in the Special Education Identification Process

The basic process is the same for identifying, placing and programming for special needs students, but the terminology varies. If there is more than one term, alternatives follow in brackets.

- Referral
- Assessment
- Eligibility meeting
- Individual education plan written and implemented
- Yearly review

Referral

Students Entering School with an Already Diagnosed Condition
When a child with an already diagnosed special need enters the school system, arrangements are usually made at the time of registration for a transition meeting with parents and school staff. Parents share information and documents with the school, the child goes on a school tour if appropriate, and arrangements are made so the child's entry to school is as smooth as possible. Even if the child already has a medical diagnosis, a formal identification by the school district will be made shortly after the child begins school. See "Eligibility Meeting" on page 122.

Students Already in School Who are Experiencing Difficulty and May Be in Need of Special Education Services
Most often, it is a parent who notices that there is something "not quite right" with their child. Sometimes it is just a feeling, sometimes a series of observations that indicate a problem, whether small or severe. In the case of severe special needs, medical and educational intervention begins even before the child starts school. At times, it is only when a younger sibling begins to surpass an older one in terms of milestones and accomplishments that parents understand that there is a problem with their child.

The classroom teacher is another person who is likely to identify the fact that a child is having difficulty. When a teacher suspects or observes a problem, she will first try a variety of accommodations in the classroom to help the student (see "Accommodations, Modifications and Alternative Programs" on pages 116–117).

The classroom teacher will also contact the parents, express her concerns, consult with the parents on strategies and or share information. If the child continues to struggle, the teacher will then meet with a Special Education teacher and or other staff within the school to determine a course of action.

Assessment

The school may recommend an assessment by a medical doctor as well as a psychoeducational assessment. An assessment can identify conditions such as learning disabilities or giftedness, but autism spectrum disorders, ADHD (Attention Deficit Hyperactivity Disorder) ODD (Oppositional Defiant Disorder) or emotional problems require diagnosis by a medical doctor. In addition to a medical and or psychoeducational assessment, other assessments may be recommended as appropriate (for example, speech and language or hearing assessment). Parents must consent before any assessment is done.

The purpose of an assessment is to identify the student's areas of strength and weakness and to determine what actions and or services are required.

The child is assessed by a qualified clinician in a number of private sessions. The clinician takes a medical and educational history from the parents. The process of assessment is usually completed over the course of two to four private sessions with the child. The clinician tests the child in the following areas:

- **Psychological:** includes intelligence, memory, processing
- **Academic:** includes reading, writing, math

Sometimes parents and classroom teachers are asked to fill in a questionnaire to share their observations of the child. The clinician compiles all the information into a report.

Be aware that the wait time for assessment can be very lengthy, sometimes as long as several years. In such cases, the child usually receives the appropriate accommodations or modifications to the program during the waiting period. If your child is waiting for an assessment, check in regularly with the school to be sure that things are moving along as quickly as possible.

Parents can choose to have an assessment done by an outside agency but should make sure that the results will be accepted by the school and school district. Assessment by an outside agency can also be costly—from several hundred to several thousand dollars.

Child Support Worker (also called Special Education Assistant, Instructional Aide, or ERW—Educational Resource Worker)

A support worker may be assigned to work with your child to support academic, physical, personal care, safety or other needs. The support worker works directly with students, helps reinforce academic concepts, takes part in home–school communication and works closely with the classroom teacher. The support worker is knowledgable about the needs of identified students and is an important part of the child's team.

Eligibility Meeting

The exact makeup of the meeting team can vary by school district, but it will usually consist of:

- parents. (If you are a single parent you may invite someone to accompany you to the meeting. If you require translation services they will be provided to you.)
- classroom teacher
- a representative of the school district
- Special Education personnel, including someone who will explain test results
- others who are involved in the child's program (for example, speech and language pathologist, school psychologist, social worker, support worker)
- an outside representative may attend the meeting or provide written recommendations or reports, if the child is receiving services from outside the school board.

During the meeting the results of the psychoeducational and other testing will be given. The results will also be accompanied by recommendations for parents and teachers regarding the child's areas of strength and weakness, academic goals, suggested accommodations or modifications to the curriculum, strategies for parents, teachers and the child to implement, and the child's best learning style.

The purpose of the eligibility meeting is to flag the student as a child with special needs, to gain access to special programs and services, and to guarantee the right to review the child's needs annually. Formal identification is to help the child be successful at school and to ensure support, not to label your child or pigeonhole him. A determination will be made whether your child is eligible for Special Education services. If your child is eligible, a placement will be made and an IEP will be written. (In some places the IEP is written after the meeting, but must be completed and implemented within 30 days.)

Placement options for Special Ed students are:

- regular classroom with support/consultation provided to the classroom teacher, but not directly to the student
- regular classroom with special instruction by a Special Education teacher in the classroom (individual or in small groups)
- regular classroom with withdrawal for instruction by a Special Education teacher (usually less than half the school day)
- integration into a regular classroom. (The child spends most of the day in a classroom with a Special Education teacher, but is integrated into a regular classroom for a portion of the day.)
- self-contained classroom. (The child is in a special classroom with a Special Education teacher and children with similar needs.)
- self-contained specialized classroom in a school other than the child's home school

The student-teacher ratio for Special Education classes is significantly lower than that of a regular classroom, but varies by school district.

Integration and Withdrawal

As there are many different placement options for students with special needs, integration and withdrawal time will depend on many factors such as the timetable of the Special Education teacher and the needs of the child. Determining factors considered are:

- how much regular classroom time the child can handle
- behavioral or emotional needs (these may vary from day to day)
- academic needs (if student requires an individual or small group lesson)
- if student requires a quiet place to write a test

When there is a special event such as a class trip, whole school assembly, guest speaker, presentation of speeches or skits in the classroom, track and field day, the timetable is flexible and special education students participate with their homeroom classmates. Children in a self-contained special education class are often "bundled up" with regular class students for participation in special events.

To make an informed decision about placement it is important that you fully understand the options. If a self-contained classroom is being considered, ask to visit the class before the placement meeting. Talk to the teacher of the self-contained class, your child's classroom teacher, Special Education staff and other parents if possible.

In most places, a child has a right to be educated in his home school. Some parents prefer to have their special needs child in the same school as his siblings. Check the regulations in your area.

A summary of the eligibility meeting will be written up and distributed to all parties. Parents are asked to sign the form, indicating whether they agree with the recommendations of the team. If parents disagree with the placement or recommendations they may withhold their signatures. There is an appeal process that enables parents to request another eligibility meeting or bring their concerns to an appeal board composed of people who have no prior knowledge of the case.

Individual Education Program or Plan (IEP) Is Written and Implemented

An IEP is a written plan that lays out program goals for the child. It includes:

- the classification of the exceptionality
- a description of the child's strengths, weaknesses and needs
- annual educational goals (in some places these are revised each term)
- Special Education services or equipment that are required
- a plan for administering medication, other medical needs (such as care of feeding tube or suctioning), toileting, sensory stimulation, etc.
- program accommodations or modifications necessary to meet the student's needs

The IEP will be given to you to review. Ask for clarification about anything you do not understand or are unsure of. Once the plan is put into effect, be sure you follow up to make sure your child is actually receiving all the services laid out in the plan.

Yearly Review

The IEP is reviewed on a regular basis, in some places at every reporting period. An annual review is done to make any necessary adjustments to the student's program or services. Parents are included in the yearly review meeting.

The Parent

You are the most important part of your child's support team. It is you who knows your child best and you are best qualified to advocate for your child. You provide the continuity from year to year and are the only person who knows the whole history of your child on a first-hand basis.

Advice for Parents Regarding Meetings

There are many meetings involved in the world of Special Education. Sometimes the meetings are small, with you and the school staff who work with your child. Other times, the meetings include personnel from the school board or special services. You are a very important member of the team. You are an equal in the education of your child. Don't be intimidated by a person's job title or by the terminology that is sometimes used. Everyone on the Special Education team is there to design and deliver a program that will enable your child to be successful at school. Here is some advice for parents attending meetings:

- Go around the table and ask each person to give their name and job description. Ask each person if they have personally observed and or assessed your child and what their involvement is with your child.
- Pass a picture of your child around so that people who have not met your child can put a face to a name, and to remind people who have worked with your child exactly who he is.
- Know board polices, be informed and educate yourself. Learn the process.
- Special Education has lots of terminology and "lingo." If you don't understand something, ask. Team members make every effort to explain everything, but speak up if you need clarification.
- Make sure that your child's classroom teacher and support worker (if applicable) are always present at meetings as they are the school staff who spend the most time with your child and know him best. They should be involved in all decision-making, programming and reviews.

General Advice for Parents of Children in Special Education

School Staff

- Get to know your child's teachers and support workers. Develop a mutually supportive relationship with them that features open and frequent communication.
- Work closely with the teacher and support worker. If your child is not receiving the program or services agreed upon at the IEP meeting or your child is not making progress, follow up and request another meeting to rectify the situation.
- Get to know the principal and local school trustee as well. The more people you know in the school community, the better.
- Always start with the teacher when seeking information or getting a report on your child.
- At the beginning of a new year or any time there is a change of classroom or Special Education teacher, support worker or other personnel, check in to make sure that the new person is familiar with your child's needs and program.
- If your child's teacher or support workers are changing, it is normal to feel some concern, but remember that your child gets something different from each person he works with and the new person may bring something out in your child that is new and great.

Educational

- Investigate all possible placements for your child before deciding on one.
- If your child is not making progress and or meetings with staff are not resolving issues, assert yourself and insist that an effective solution be found.
- Special needs children have a right to be in the school and a right to an education suited to their needs. Don't settle for less.
- Know your child's program and the specifics of what they are learning, as well as what the rest of the children in the class are learning.
- The regular conference at report card time is usually not sufficient to review your child's progress. Schedule longer interviews at more frequent intervals.

Organizational Hints
- Be sure to keep excellent records. Take notes and keep all paperwork.
- When you write a letter or e-mail regarding your child's education, send a copy to everyone on the team.
- Check in regularly to be sure there is communication between the classroom teacher and the Special Education teacher to ensure that agendas, notes and classroom materials are making it from one class to the other.
- Follow up with the classroom teacher, Special Education teacher and even the child himself to be sure he is receiving all the services to which he is entitled.

Personal
- The teachers, support workers and Special Education contacts at school will change over the years, but you are always there. Take pride in your role as your child's chief supporter and advocate.
- If at all possible, both parents should attend meetings and present a united front.
- Be polite, approachable and open-minded, and expect the same of the education professionals you work with.
- Develop a network including other parents, professionals, advocacy organizations, etc. Keep in touch with those people.
- Sometimes you may have to fight for what your child needs. Many years later you may still be fighting battles. Advocate. Never give up. Know that you are a pioneer and though you are working for your child, you are also paving the way for future parents and children.

Early Intervention

As parents, we want everything to be smooth going for our children. It is a difficult thing to face and admit that there is a problem with your child. But when problems do arise, it is best to deal with them right away. Many problems, both severe and mild, reach a quicker and happier resolution with early intervention. When parents work together with medical professionals and educators, a team approach is formed that can benefit your child.

Acceptance

Acceptance of a child's special needs can be a very emotional and difficult thing and can take a long time. You are not alone. There are many families going through the same experiences as you are. Most teachers have been through the process many times with many families and are more than willing to talk to you, to walk you through the process involved and to make suggestions to help you feel supported.

You can also seek help through a network of other parents or organized associations that offer support and assistance to special needs children and their families. These associations often have guest speakers and seminars to help you learn about your child's diagnosis and ensure you are getting the best possible help for your child. Your family doctor may also have some suggestions on ways you can educate yourself.

As difficult as it may be, try to be positive about your child's challenges. Realize that there are a lot of people working on your child's behalf. Take things one step at a time.

Most parents leave no stone unturned in an effort to help their child. Talk to people, read, investigate strategies and programs, and keep working until your child has the services and supports that will enable him to achieve success—whether it be in small steps or leaps and bounds.

What Teachers Want Parents to Know

Some parents are too meek and mild and, perhaps, are intimidated in group meetings or afraid to disagree with an "expert." Don't be afraid to ask questions, express your opinions or contribute to discussions.

Some parents are too forceful and see the school team as "the enemy." Know that everyone is working in the best interest of your child and that working as a team will get the best results for him.

Some parents want help for their child, but they don't want the child labeled, removed from class or centered out in any way.

Teachers are skilled at making accommodations for children without drawing attention to them. However, some programs can only be delivered effectively in a quiet small group or individual setting.

Always keep in mind that you are not alone. There are knowledgable and compassionate people to help you navigate the system. Ask for help if you are struggling or unhappy.

There is a fine balance involved in being an advocate for your child—trust the expertise of the school personnel, but make sure your input is heard and trust your instincts too.

It could be that a classroom teacher has not had personal experience with your child's type of exceptionality. Make yourself available to share information and educate the teacher and fellow classmates. The first-hand information that you share will help the teacher get to know your child and his needs quickly and to become adept at programming for and working with him.

Celebrate successes. Whether your child has completed a project, made eye contact with his teacher, exercised self-control or spoken a word, celebrate. Each step is important, each step is a milestone, each step is a triumph.

Special Equipment and Assistive Devices

Schools provide special equipment and assistive devices for students with special needs. For example, students who are hearing impaired often make use of an FM system. The teacher and student both wear a headset and the teacher's voice is transmitted to the student over a radio frequency. Other types of assistive devices and technology for students include voice-recognition software, special computer keyboards (for example, with larger keys and easy touch), glare-reduction screens, picture symbol programs for non-verbal students, large-type books and carpeted floor to reduce ambient noise. Most schools are equipped to handle students with physical needs. Wheelchair ramps, handicapped washrooms and elevators are commonly found in all but the oldest schools.

Children with special needs require individualized instruction. There is a process to follow to ensure that every student gets the required services, equipment and curriculum he or she needs to enjoy success at school.

- Special needs are classified by the type of exceptionality
- Each eligible special needs student has a specific learning plan called an IEP that outlines individualized learning goals
- Parents are an integral part of the child's Special Education team and need to advocate for their child

Chapter 11

Report Cards and Parent-Teacher Conferences

"She systematically describes locations of objects or people using positional language."

This was an actual comment on a first grader's report card. Do you have any idea what it means? Do you know what subject this comment is referring to? If not, you are not alone. (The comment above means the child can tell if she is in front of or behind someone, first in line or last in line, and the subject is Math.) It can sometimes be challenging to wade through educational jargon to seek the answer to the simple question "How is my child doing at school?"

Parent groups have been questioning the baffling language used in report card comments for years.

A report card is a written evaluation of a student's progress. Formats for report cards are not widely standardized as there are many types of school systems, each with its own reporting procedure. Even within a single school system, different grade levels can have different reporting methods. Curriculum is ever changing. As a result, there are many types of report cards and grading systems. No wonder parents can be baffled by their child's report card.

All report cards cover two main areas:

• academic achievement
• learning skills (encompassing social, behavioral, work habits, use of time, co-operation with others, work completion, conflict resolution, participation and effort)

Report cards are usually divided in two sections: marks, or grades, and comments. The comments are sometimes standardized and teachers merely select the comment that matches the child's performance. Often, they sound like the opening comment in this chapter—impersonal, stilted and clinical. In certain areas of the report card, teachers are sometimes free to express the child's progress, strengths and weaknesses using their own words.

Sample Grading Systems

Letter Grades and Percentages

A = 80–100%
B = 70–79%
C = 60–69%
D = 50–59%
F = 0–49%

Levels

Level 4 = A
Level 3 = B
Level 2 = C
Level 1 = D
Level 0 = F

Letter Grades

E = Excellent
G = Good
S = Satisfactory
N = Needs Improvement

Checklist

✔ Listen to stories without interrupting
✔ Cut with scissors
✔ Manage bathroom needs
✔ Button shirts, pants, coats, and zip up zippers
✔ Count to ten
✔ Bounce a ball

Performance is indicated with a checkmark. The child has either mastered the task or is still developing the skills to master the task.

Standardized Comments

These comments accompany the mark for each subject. The teacher chooses them from a preexisting list. They are factual and impersonal. Each child who earned a B in the subject would get the exact same comment. Only the names are different.

For example: Jane Doe demonstrates considerable effectiveness in understanding the geographic concepts and techniques and can apply them to her assignments.

Anecdotal Comments

Anecdotal comments often accompany the mark for each subject. They are written by the teacher in his or her own words and are personalized comments about your child's progress based on observation.

For example: Jane Doe is able to skip count by twos, fives and tens up to 100 and understands how this process works.

Some report cards have a section where teachers can write general and personal anecdotal comments about your child.

For example: You can't help but smile when Jane Doe is around.

Reports for a Student with an IEP

In the report card of a student with an Individual Education Plan (IEP), the student is evaluated according to individual learning expectations that may vary from grade level expectations. A regular report card form is used and it indicates that the student has an IEP. Special needs students who follow an alternative curriculum and cannot be graded using traditional methods are given an anecdotal report card that contains comments only.

How Teachers Assess Students

Teachers assess students on an ongoing basis during any unit of study.

Diagnostic (or pre-) assessment can occur before a concept is taught. It indicates a child's level of existing knowledge on a given topic and can give a teacher an idea of how much or what type of instruction is needed.

Formative assessment is done during the learning process. It is not used for evaluation, but provides students with feedback and opportunities for practice. This type of assessment gives teachers information as to what learning opportunities students require.

Summative (or cumulative) assessment is done after a concept has been taught and practiced. It allows teachers to evaluate a student's achievement in a given unit of study.

Assessment Tools

Teachers use multiple assessment tools such as:
- checklists
- informal observations
- conferencing with students
- rubrics or marking schemes

- tests or exams
- oral presentations
- portfolios
- performance tasks
- self and peer evaluations
- response journals or logs
- creative performances
- observing student interaction with others

Assessments are increasingly focused on measuring both the finished product produced by the student and the thought processes that went into the creation of the product.

Many school districts provide teachers with exemplars, which are samples of student work at each level of achievement. The exemplars clearly spell out the criteria for each level.

When the Report Card Arrives Home

When your child arrives home with her report card, read it over and then spend a few minutes going over and reading it with your child. Be positive and praise your child for any good marks and positive comments. Ask your child what she thinks about the report, what she is most proud of and how she thinks she can improve.

In our classrooms, we used to have our students fill in a blank report card form for themselves. It was amazing how well most students intuitively knew their own strengths and weaknesses. Your child may be able to bring an interesting insight into your discussion.

Talk about any problem areas or poor marks. This is not the moment to come up with a game plan for improvement. Take time on report card day to focus on, and celebrate, successes and begin fresh the next day with plans for improvement.

Avoid the temptation of comparing a child's report card with that of her brothers, sisters, cousins or friends. Applaud the unique achievements and special talents of each child. Some families like to celebrate report card successes with a family outing or treat.

It sometimes happens that children in the same family have very different report cards. It is important for parents to speak with each child privately about the report card and for the parent and the child to come up with a plan for improvement that can be discussed with the teacher at the conference. Remember that a child who is getting top marks still has areas in which she can improve and a child with poor marks still has areas of strength. Each child in your family will have the satisfaction and pride of being acknowledged for those strengths and the challenge of striving to improve.

How Are Report Card Marks Given?

It is important for you and your child to understand that the marks on the report card are the marks your child earned. Many riled parents have come to the school growling, "Who can I talk to about this mark?" to which our favorite principal's reply was always, "Talk to your kid!"

If you or your child feel that a mark has been unfairly assigned and you want to know how the mark was arrived at, feel free to ask. Be aware that assessment and evaluation are very regulated and follow a specific process. The final mark is not based solely on one test or assignment. Many factors are taken into consideration when assessing student performance, such as tests, projects, presentations, group work, homework completion, participation and daily class work. The mark is not simply a teacher's impression of your child's achievement.

For example: your child is a star athlete on sports teams outside of school, but receives a lower-than-A+ mark in Physical Education.

It could be that your child has a lot of ability, but has not demonstrated the specific skills required in the curriculum and he brags, hogs the ball and shows off. The teacher is grading on more than "he shoots, he scores." Skills such as teamwork and respectful behavior toward teammates are also taken into consideration.

For example: your child got 90% on the Science test, but only a B in Science on the report card. It could be that her marks in other areas of the Science curriculum that term were not as high. When the 90% test mark was averaged in with note taking, assignments, impromptu tests, participation, homework completion and presentations, the resulting final mark was a B.

For example: occasionally there is no mark given or N/A (not applicable) appears for a certain subject on a report card. It could be that teachers are not required to report on all strands of Math each term or that Science is taught in one term and Social Studies in another term. It sometimes happens that there is a computer glitch. Check with the teacher if you have questions.

Interpreting the Report Card

Yes, the simple question that parents want the answer to is: "How is my child doing at school?" This question is, in fact, answered in the report card, but it is sometimes hidden beneath layers of jargon. It can therefore be difficult to get a simple, clear answer. The parent-teacher conference is an opportunity to get answers to specific questions regarding the report card and to "cut to the chase" in simple layman's terms.

If you find the report card hard to interpret, know that it is not designed to deliberately stump you. School districts have implemented report cards with standardized comments in part to answer parent requests for more accountability, and to provide a more in-depth description of exactly what is being taught. In some districts, this has resulted in sentences containing a lot of comparative adjectives and descriptors that many parents have told us sound like "gobbledygook." The combination of the report card and the parent-teacher interview should allow you to get answers to all your questions, to understand your child's strengths and areas for improvement, and to know how you can best support your child's learning at home.

After you have read the report card carefully, spoken with your child about it, made a list of questions and concerns, and made an appointment for the parent-teacher conference, you are ready for the next stage of the process.

Reacting to the Report Card

Whatever your child's marks are on any report card, they should not come as a shock to you. Teachers are trained and instructed to make early contact with parents if an academic or behavioral problem arises. Parents should be aware of a child's progress by seeing the marks on tests and assignments that the child has completed and brought home (usually requiring the parent's signature), looking over homework, signing the agenda or homework book, and conversing with the child. Parents are responsible for making contact with the teacher if they have concerns about the child's progress.

In all cases, the report card must be tempered by your knowledge of your own child. If the marks are not stellar, but your child has worked hard and tried her very best, she deserves recognition for what she has achieved. Remember that very few children excel in all subject areas and not all children are capable of top marks. Likewise, if your child has satisfactory marks, but you know that she could be scoring higher marks, this must be acknowledged, pointed out to the child and acted upon.

If your child has areas in which she needs significant improvement, ask your child what she thinks she needs to do, both at home and at school in order to get better marks. Share your own comments and observations, and make a preliminary plan with your child. At the parent-teacher conference, the plan can be finalized with input from the teacher.

After you have read the report card and talked with your child, jot down any questions or concerns that you want to discuss with the teacher. This will be your "talk list" for the parent-teacher conference. It will help guide and focus the discussion and prevent you from forgetting anything.

If you feel that a teacher routinely assigns marks that "leave room for improvement" in subsequent terms, or you feel that the teacher is an "easy" or "hard" marker, address these concerns directly with the teacher.

Different marks in different terms do not necessarily mean that the child is not working hard or that her level of effort has decreased. Each reporting period is different, with different course material covered. So, while your child may bring home an A in Math one term (for Geometry), a B- the next term in Algebra reflects only the child's achievement in that strand of mathematics. It does not mean that the child is slipping in Math, rather that one strand presented more of a challenge.

What Happens After?

Most report cards have a section for parent signature, comments and a request for a parent-teacher conference. Almost all parents sign the report card and make an appointment for an interview, but in our experience, only a few take the time to fill out the comment section. This is an opportunity for you to provide written feedback to your child's teacher. It is another way to keep the lines of communication open between home and school.

Schools have various systems for booking parent-teacher conferences. Some schools ask parents to fill in a form indicating the day and time period that is best for a conference, and each teacher books his or her own appointments. Other schools have a central chart and book conference times by phone. Consideration is usually given to large families so that conference times are coordinated and the parents don't have to come to the school at three or four different times. There is also a wide variation in the times of conferences. Some schools offer conferences in the evenings, some during a Professional Activity Day (no school for children) and some offer a series of evenings.

Parent-teacher conference day (or night) is a very busy time for teachers. Conferences are usually booked one after the other, sometimes from the time school ends until 8:00 p.m. or 9:00 p.m., with a short dinner break. Conferences are usually scheduled for 10- to 20-minute intervals. It is important to be on time for your appointment so you don't keep the next family waiting and put the whole schedule behind. Be sure to call the school office to cancel your appointment if you cannot make it.

The Parent-Teacher Conference

Meeting with the teacher will provide you with answers to your questions as well as a chance to hear the teacher's more informal comments on your child's progress in a give-and-take conversation. It provides a better understanding of the "big picture" of your child's progress, as a written report can only convey a certain amount of information.

If your schedule does not allow you to meet with the teacher during regular conference times, call and try to arrange a different time. Teachers realize that not all parents are able to attend interviews during regularly scheduled times and will make every effort to accommodate you.

Some parents feel that if their child is doing well there is nothing to discuss with the teacher, and so they do not attend the conference. You should try to meet with the teacher even if your child is getting top marks and you have no concerns. It signals to your child that you are very interested in her education and that you and the teacher are partners, along with her, in her education. A child who is doing well is often very excited to have her parents and her teacher meet and to bask a little in the positive comments that are made.

If you are attending the conference together with your spouse or with the child's other parent, step-parent or guardian, be sure you touch base with that person beforehand to agree on what you want to say, ask and discuss with the teacher. If you and the other adult do not agree on issues regarding your child's education, at least resolve to do so in a calm way. There have been some awkward situations in which a teacher is sitting with two adults who are arguing with each other instead of focusing on the achievement of the child. Another option is to request separate interviews.

Should Your Child Attend the Parent-Teacher Interview?

Whether or not you should take your child to the conference is a question that is sometimes addressed by the school or is sometimes left to your discretion. Parent-teacher conferences with the child present can be very productive, particularly in the case of an older student. If recommendations are being made for the student to follow, then the student should be present and be an active participant in making and implementing of the plan.

What You Can Learn from the Conference

Most parent-teacher conferences take place right in the classroom. Being in your child's class gives you a chance to see your child's desk (likely cleaned up especially for this occasion), displays of student work around the classroom and a feel for the place where your child spends several hours each day. Looking at the work displayed in the class can give you an idea of where your child's work fits in relative to the work of other children. For example, you may notice that most children's work is neat and tidy and your child's is messy, or that most children's stories are one page long and your child's story is three pages long.

Teachers have samples of your child's work to show you and talk about. Often there is an entire portfolio of work that has been selected both by your child and the teacher. Different types of work are reflected in the portfolio: artwork, writing journals, graphs and charts, projects, etc. The work demonstrates your child's achievement and effort in various curriculum areas over a period of time. In some schools, parent-teacher conferences begin with a short presentation by the student. The child presents pieces of work from her school portfolio to her parents, commenting and elaborating on what she has learned. The teacher adds her comments by referring to the portfolio work and the report card.

Teachers often follow a formula in parent-teacher conferences. They start by talking about something positive (strengths), then speak about any issues or areas for improvement (weaknesses) and then end on a positive note (next steps). You may wish to follow this formula as well when speaking to the teacher.

What Should You Discuss with the Teacher?

When speaking with the teacher, feel free to talk about both academic and non-academic skills. Sharing your child's talents and interests outside the classroom can give the teacher a fuller understanding. If you have a shy child or one who doesn't talk a lot, the interview can be a good opportunity to find out from the teacher who your child's friends are and what he is really like when he is away from you. You can also give your child's teacher updates on any events and changes, happy or otherwise, that may be affecting her student's performance. Many parents want to discuss homework — some think their child has too much, others think there is not enough. These are all valid topics for discussion.

If you have concerns, bring them up early in the conference. Most conferences are scheduled for 10 to 20 minutes at the most. If you wait until the last moment there will not be sufficient time to talk about your concern and decide on a plan of action.

In a small number of cases a second interview may be required. It could be that you have a lot to discuss and you simply run out of time. In rare circumstances, parents are not satisfied with the outcome of the conference. In this case, another meeting should be set up, possibly with the principal in attendance. Most interviews are very successful and solid parent-teacher relationships are formed, much to the benefit of your child.

When the parent-teacher conference is done, file your child's report card in a special place. You may wish or need to access it when the next report card comes out, in case of a move or when your child is grown up and a parent herself, and you pull out those old report cards to show your grandchildren what their mother or father was like as a kid.

The report card is a formal written evaluation of your child's progress. Different school districts use different grading systems and report card formats. When your child brings her report card home:

- Read over the report card
- Reread and discuss it with your child
- Offer praise for work well done
- Help the child accept responsibility for her marks and make a plan for improvement
- Don't compare the reports of siblings
- Make a list of questions and concerns to discuss at the parent teacher conference

When preparing for a parent-teacher conference:

- Make an appointment
- Bring the report card and a list of questions to the conference
- Be on time
- Call the school and cancel if you cannot attend
- Reschedule the appointment if need be

Chapter 12
Conflict Resolution

It is inevitable that children will experience conflict in the elementary school years, both at home and at school. Our job as parents is to equip our children to handle conflict and its repercussions.

Most conflicts at school are not "life threatening, morally threatening or unhealthy," as parenting guru Barbara Coloroso says. That said, serious conflicts and situations do exist, must be dealt with immediately and require adult intervention. As for the more common, everyday situations, the goal is to enable your child to resolve problems as independently as possible.

Most of the conflicts we deal with at school are student–student: in the hall, in the classroom, on the bus and in the yard. With hundreds of kids in one place, there are bound to be disagreements. They range from the serious (hitting) to the ridiculous ("he looked at me!"). In most cases, conflicts are minor and the solutions relatively easy.

The strategies teachers use in problem solving and conflict resolution at school can be tailored and used equally effectively at home. At school, there is a gradual release of responsibility. Initially, the teacher is the mediator and walks the children through these steps. Next, the teacher might oversee the two children as they try to work out a solution. The eventual goal is for the children to solve their own problem without adult intervention.

Steps for Solving Conflicts between Children

1. Be calm and have the children cool off.
2. Find a private spot to talk.
3. Ask each child to tell you what happened. Each has a turn without interruption. No yelling, no insulting, no rude language.
4. Have each child restate what the other has said.
5. Have each child take responsibility for his actions. In most conflicts, both parties are partly at fault.
6. Help the children figure out the underlying problem.
7. Ask the children to suggest possible solutions that both parties agree to, for example, taking turns, sharing, working together, staying apart, doing a different activity altogether.
8. Have the children choose the solution that works best for both of them and implement it.
9. Have the children apologize to each other.
10. Follow up later to see if the situation has improved.

Helping Your Child Deal with Conflict

When your child is upset by a problem at school, the first instinct of many parents is to jump in, contact the teacher and "fix it." Be aware that some children may be afraid to face conflict on their own and will try to maneuver you into acting on their behalf. If you jump in to save the day, you miss an important, teachable moment. By helping children plan and implement strategies, you are equipping them with problem-solving skills for life.

When your child has confided in you about a problem that is upsetting to her, it is natural that you will be upset too. The first step in effective troubleshooting is to remain calm and take a deep breath. If your child is angry or agitated, help her to calm down as well. The next step is to simply listen to your child—in private. Get her to tell you, in detail, what has happened. When listening to your child, know that you are hearing the truth as she sees it. By nature, young children are self-centered. Not in a selfish way, but because they have not yet developed the ability to see and understand other people's viewpoints. It is your job to help them understand that there are two sides to every story.

Ask the Right Questions

Do not prompt her with leading questions such as, "What did that mean girl say to you?" and "Hasn't she hurt your feelings enough?" A good strategy to elicit accurate information from your child is to ask, "If I were looking through the window in your classroom and you didn't know I was there, would I see exactly what you are telling me?" Making notes will help you keep the facts straight. Here are some questions we have used with students:

- What is the problem?
- Why do you think this has happened?
- Is there anyone else involved?
- Is this the first time this has happened or is this an on-going issue?
- What part of this problem are you responsible for?
- Is there anything you are doing that is causing this problem?
- Is there anything you are not doing that is causing this problem?
- Is there something that you should be doing?
- Is there anything you are doing that is aggravating the situation?
- How have you tried to solve this problem?
- What are some other ways you could make things better?

Figuring out a Strategy or Coping Technique

The next step is to help the child come up with strategy, a coping technique and or an appropriate solution to implement at school the next day. Follow up and keep track of how things are going. If the problem is not solved and the conflict continues, you need to contact the teacher. This is the time for you to intervene and get involved.

School Rules and Consequences

Each school has its own code of conduct, which lays out expectations for inappropriate behavior. Most schools use a progressive discipline system, meaning that the consequences escalate depending on the severity and frequency of the incidents. The consequences might progress in this way:

- discussion and verbal reprimand
- an account of the problem and proposed solutions written by the student (sometimes called a "think paper")
- detention
- parent contact
- removal of privileges
- in-school suspension
- at-home suspension
- expulsion

For more on school rules and consequences see Chapter 9.

When Are Parents Called?

If your child is involved in a serious issue at school—for example, violent behavior or smoking—the school will notify you right away. For less serious infractions, the school tries to handle discipline internally. Repeated incidents will result in a call home.

Your child's classroom teacher may call you if there is an academic or behavioral concern. Teachers usually address issues early before they escalate.

You may also receive a call from a teacher to report good news. Maybe your child has shown great improvement in a subject area; your child did something outstanding, such as helping another child in need; your child has shown a positive change in attitude and behavior; or your child has said something funny that the teacher wants to share with you. One of our favorites was the child who said, "My great grandfather got shot in the war, but he knew how to limbo so he didn't get killed."

Solving Student–Teacher Conflicts

If you find yourself in a position where your child has a conflict with the teacher and she is not making any headway toward a solution on her own, your intervention may be required.

When both you and your child are calm, have a discussion about the problem. Ask your child to tell you all the details of what has happened. Document what has transpired.

However tempted you might be to go directly to the principal, start with the teacher. Make an appointment and let the teacher know what it is you want to discuss. You will have prepared and made notes, so give the teacher a chance to do likewise. When all parties are prepared and make an honest effort, it leads to a more organized and productive discussion.

Nobody, including children, parents and teachers, wants a problem hanging over their head. Know that the vast majority of teachers are as ready, willing and able to solve problems and resolve situations as are most parents. But sometimes, for whatever reason, an unpleasant conflict arises that is very difficult to deal with.

You can decide if you want your young child present during the discussion with the teacher. If your child is in the upper grades, it is highly recommended that she be a participant in this three-way discussion. This is the best way to ensure that the whole truth comes out. Each hears first-hand what the others have to say.

At the meeting, remember to shake hands, introduce yourself, be calm, speak politely, and be assertive but not aggressive, especially if your child is present. You are your child's role model in all things, including how you handle difficult situations. You should expect the same from the teacher. Just as you want the teacher to hear what you have to say, you need to listen to what the teacher is saying. Really listen. The teacher will be sharing her version of events, which may differ from what your child has told you.

If the meeting results in a positive, give-and-take discussion, a solution to the problem may be discovered and can be implemented.

If you feel nervous and are thinking, "I am concerned that if I tell you everything that is on my mind it will make things worse for my child," go ahead and say that. You are doing this to help your child. You have opened up to the teacher and now it is the teacher's turn to respond in kind. In the same way that it was difficult for you to speak up, the teacher may have things to share that are difficult for her to say—and for you to hear. Once all the information is out in the open, perhaps it will be easier to arrive at a solution. On the other hand it is possible that no solution can be reached.

If, at any time, things get out of hand, voices are raised, accusations are hurled and the focus is lost, either you or the teacher have the right to end the discussion.

Involving the Principal

If no solution can be reached, it is time to involve the principal. Make an appointment and let the principal know what it is you want to discuss. Make it clear that you have already met with the teacher. The principal will facilitate a meeting between you and the teacher. In all likelihood, a solution can be reached at this level.

The solution to most problems can be found at school level. Very rarely do problems need to be brought to the attention of the supervisory officer or other school board personnel. Parents who attempt to bypass the teacher or principal and go "above their heads" are referred back to the school level, as protocol was not followed. There are some problems, however, that necessitate the involvement of the supervisory officer.

Extreme Measures

It sometimes happens, despite repeated attempts to resolve a problem, that no solution can be reached and the child is still suffering. As a result, the whole family suffers. Parents are then faced with a very tough decision: to leave the child in the existing situation or to move the child to a different school. There are no guarantees a move will improve the situation.

Possible Reasons for Problems or Conflicts

Here are some examples of problems and conflicts that could arise at school. It is important to pinpoint the exact cause. The following scenarios are all possibilities. Once you understand the cause of the problem or conflict, you are better equipped to find a solution. There is no "one size fits all" solution. Make a plan and follow it through.

Your child starts a new grade and in a short time her marks plummet. She is unhappy at school about her marks and with her teacher, and this unhappiness spills over into the home.

- It could be that the teacher has a different philosophy, stricter standards and a tougher marking scheme than the previous teacher.
- It could be that your child has entered a new division with a more challenging, in-depth curriculum and needs to adjust to the new requirements and heavier workload.
- It could be that there is a change in your child's social dynamics (for example, the child develops "the friends are everything" mentality, has raging hormones, is being ostracized by friends, is being bullied, etc.) with the result that schoolwork is suffering.
- It could be that something going on at home is affecting your child's performance in the classroom.
- It could be that your child is not working to his potential.
- It could be that the teacher is struggling or ineffectual.

Your child is struggling in a particular subject at school.

- It could be that your child has not grasped a certain concept within the subject area and requires extra help, re-teaching and or additional practice.
- It could be that your child has a fear or a mental block regarding the subject.
- It could be that there is an obstacle such as a learning problem or disability and a learning plan is needed.
- It could be that your child has developed a defeatist "I can't do this" attitude and is not focusing on the subject.

You are hearing from your child that he is constantly being picked on, blamed and centered out by the teacher.

- It could be that it is the beginning of a new school year and your child has not yet adjusted to the new teacher and perceives any suggestions from the teacher as harsh criticism.
- It could that there is a social dynamic situation (for example, your child has linked up with one or more friends and together they are acting out in class) resulting in the need for frequent redirection from the teacher.
- It could be that the teacher and your child are rubbing each other the wrong way.

- It could be that something is going on at home and it is affecting the child in one of two ways: the child is turning inward and does not want to be called upon in class, or the child is acting out and requires frequent teacher attention.
- It could be that the teacher is, in fact, picking on your child.
- It could be that the teacher is struggling or ineffectual and picking on everybody.

Struggling or Ineffectual Teacher

If your child has a struggling or ineffectual teacher, document your concerns based on what your child has told you and what you have observed. Meet with the teacher to discuss these concerns. It could be that the problem is temporary. The teacher could be experiencing ill health, a death in the family, a family crisis or could be new to the profession or grade. If time passes and there is no improvement, arrange to meet with the principal.

In any profession there are people who are not well suited to their job and don't do a good job. Unfortunately, it is the same in teaching. If, after meeting with the teacher and principal, there is no resolution and the problems continue you will be faced with three choices:

- Leave your child in the class and equip him with coping strategies.
- Ask for your child to be moved to another class. This is not always possible as there may only be one teacher for that grade or it is not school policy.
- Change schools. This is an extreme measure and you will have to weigh the pros and cons carefully.

Every year, every single teacher is telling you that there is an issue (academic, behavioral or social) with your child.

- It could be that this ongoing problem that has not been handled effectively by the school requiring a team approach and better communication between home and school to resolve the issue.
- It could be that every single teacher has been wrong about your child.
- It could be that you are in denial and there is a issue with your child that you have already been made aware of, but have chosen to ignore.

It appears that the teacher does not like your child.
- It could be that it is your child's perception and not the actual case. If a child's previous teacher was "the best teacher in the whole world," a new teacher can seem lacking by comparison.
- It could be that the teacher is not a "warm, fuzzy" person and keeps all students at arm's length.
- It could be that the teacher does not, in fact, like your child.

Your child does not like the teacher.
- It could be that the teacher is strict and demanding.
- It could be that the teacher is not a "warm, fuzzy" person.
- It could be that your child simply does not like the teacher and there is, in fact, a personality conflict.

Personality Conflicts

There are situations where there is really and truly a personality conflict between student and teacher. Like it or not, personality conflicts exist and are a fact of life experienced by people of all ages in families, schools, workplaces and in the community. If there is no harm being done and the child's marks are not affected, the best you can do is help your child develop coping skills to get along with the teacher, as they have a whole school year to get through together.

In rare circumstances, your child may experience a teacher who does not like her and shows it. In this situation, the teacher is the grownup and bears the responsibility for managing the relationship. Unfortunately, this is not always the case. A "cards on the table" meeting is in order.

Your child is in conflict with another child or a group of children.
- It could be that there has been a one-time incident between your child and another child.
- It could be that there is an ongoing clash of personalities between your child and another child.
- It could be that there has been a blow-up between your child and a good friend or group of friends resulting in "You're not my friend any more."
- It could be that there has been a physical altercation between your child and another child.

See Chapter 13 for information on peer pressure and bullying.

Suspected or Actual Abuse

The most important consideration is the safety of the child. If, at any time, you have reasonable cause to believe that a child is being sexually or physically abused by a teacher, school employee or another student, **act immediately.** Seek medical help if necessary and contact police or social services. The choice is yours whether or not you contact the school principal directly. One resource is Childhelp National Child Abuse Hotline at 1-800-4-A-CHILD. This service operates in both Canada and the United States.

Everyone experiences conflict. It is our job as parents and teachers to equip children to handle conflicts big and small as calmly and effectively as possible.

- When conflicts arise, following an established set of steps will provide the best chance for a quick and satisfactory resolution
- The goal is to provide your child with the skills to solve problems as independently as possible
- Some conflicts can be difficult for your child to solve alone and may require your intervention
- Each school has a code of conduct which lays out expectations for students and consequences for breaking the rules
- There are many reasons conflicts occur. Working through the situation and finding the root cause of the problem can be challenging, but once you have found it, you are well on your way to a solution

Chapter 13

Peer Pressure and Bullying

Attending school on a daily basis for 10 months of the year ties your child to a peer group. This group will fluctuate over the years as children move in and out of the school, but a core group remains. Unless your child changes schools, this group of children will automatically be his peer group for the duration of his elementary school years and therefore influential in his life.

Most peers are merely acquaintances. A child usually finds a friend or a small group of friends within the larger peer group. These friends hang out together, text each other, spend recesses together and visit each other's houses. The friendship is based on mutual interests, being comfortable with each other and having fun together.

A child is part of a small circle of friends as well as a larger peer group, and is influenced by both. Kids care about acceptance from both their friends and the larger peer group. They fear being rejected, don't want to be seen as "different" and just want to be liked.

Your child will experience peer pressure. It is a part of growing up and a part of life. And it doesn't end when school does. Your child will likely give in to it every now and then, which is normal. Peer pressure happens when a child feels pressure to participate in an activity or act in a certain way. A child is sometimes persuaded to follow what her friends say and do. In most cases, the trends your child follows will be as harmless as wanting the latest technological gizmo or making a fashion statement.

Peer pressure can be positive, neutral and negative, although the first two types are not usually cause for concern. It can be spoken or unspoken: things may be said directly to the child or the child may just think that she is supposed to act or dress in a certain way.

Positive Peer Pressure

A school peer group can share many wonderful experiences together, from the first day of school, class trips, extracurricular activities, assemblies, concerts, school "a-thons" through to graduation. Children experience positive peer pressure when they are inspired by their friends to:
- be nice, be honest
- work hard
- avoid situations that could result in trouble
- compete for good grades

- volunteer their services
- pursue like interests
- join a club or team
- follow the rules
- try new things
- decide not to follow those who are making poor choices
- act respectfully
- set a good example
- be a good role model

When engaging in these activities, an individual child enjoys a feeling of camaraderie, the satisfaction of teamwork, the thrill of achievement and the comfort of belonging. As a result, personal satisfaction, self-esteem and confidence are raised.

Neutral Peer Pressure

Children are greatly influenced by their peers and they want to be "part of the crowd." Kids expend a lot of energy, hard work and attention on being, and staying part of, the crowd. Neutral peer pressure is relatively harmless (although it may be expensive). It involves things like a child seeing the latest movie, listening to popular music, wearing the latest in cool clothing and owning the most up-to-date technology (and for older kids, possibly a body piercing or tattoo). As a parent, you have to decide what you can afford and will allow your child to do. Pick your battles, as you may have to take a hard line later when dealing with negative peer pressure.

Negative Peer Pressure

When the term peer pressure is used, it most often refers to negative peer pressure. Examples of negative peer pressure are situations where children are influenced to:

- disrespect authority
- go against their gut feeling
- break rules
- steal
- tell lies
- wear inappropriate clothing
- make poor choices
- gossip or spread rumors

- make fun of someone and use put-downs
- tease, harass or bully
- hurt someone
- follow blindly
- use obscene gestures or language

Giving in to negative peer pressure can result in children taking part in activities that are harmful, hurtful, damaging and even dangerous (smoking, taking drugs, carrying a weapon, sexual encounters at an early age). Nobody is actually physically forcing a person to do something, but the pressure to conform, to agree, to partake is so powerful that the child gives in.

A child who is acting under pressure may feel nervous or lacking in confidence. Sometimes they aren't sure of what to do and don't know how to get out of a difficult situation. Often, they give in, make the wrong decision and later wish that hadn't. The child then ends up feeling anxious, guilty and bad about themselves. Parents must remember that kids will make mistakes.

Children do not have the experience or mental capacity of an adult. They need guidance and explanations about why things are not good for them. For example: your child asks if she can go to her friend's house with a group of friends after school to hang out and do homework. However, the friend's parents will not be home. If you say "No," your child's next question will be, "Why not, all the other kids are going?"

Every parent has said, "Because I said so," but that does not take advantage of the "teachable" moment. By explaining your thinking, you are showing your child that decision-making is based on thought, valid reasons and an informed judgment. Instead, try saying, "I am worried about your safety" or "You are too young to be left unsupervised." Your child may not be happy with you, but you have modeled your decision-making based on sound reasoning. By repeatedly demonstrating, modeling and explaining your decisions, you child stores a bank of decision-making strategies.

You can't stop your child from experiencing peer pressure. However, there are many steps you can take and skills you can teach at home from a very early age to help her develop a strong character, which will enable her to make good choices. Character education has become a focus in many school districts in recent years through class lessons, assemblies and role-playing activities covering such topics as respect, fairness and inclusion.

Things Parents Can Do to Help Build Character

Here are some ways to work with your child in order to better equip her to deal with peer pressure.

Communication
- Carry on informal, casual conversations (as opposed to an interrogation) about her friends and activities.
- Acknowledge positive behavior without over-praising.
- Allow her vocalize her opinions and value what she says.
- Teach her to resist peer pressure by helping her develop responses such as: "No," "No thanks," and "Thanks, but I'm not into that."
- At some stages, children value the opinion of a relative or other adult more than that of their parents. Enlist the help of a special person to talk with your child.
- Get to know your child's friends and their parents.
- When your child is going out, always know where she is going and who she is with. This is all the more important as your child gets older.

Setting a Good Example
Parents need to model strong moral values for your child to follow. Through conversation and example, help your child learn to consider the consequences of her actions both for herself and for others.

Developing Values
- Teach her right from wrong and stress that it is not always easy to do what is right.
- Encourage her to listen to her "inner voice" and to make good choices on her own.
- Help your child develop the confidence to know that it's okay to like what she likes, to be an individual and not feel that she always has to conform.
- Teach your child to think before acting.
- Help your child to see things from various points of view.

Boundaries

It is important for parents to set rules and limits. You need to hold your child accountable for her behavior and teach her to take responsibility for her own actions, rather than blaming her friends.

What a Child Can Do in a Negative Peer Pressure Situation

Parents should discuss negative peer pressure situations with their child and offer them the following advice:

- Know yourself and your boundaries and what you are comfortable with.
- Ask yourself " Is this trouble?" "Is this right?" before going along with the crowd.
- Stick together with friends.
- When faced with a tough decision, remember that all decisions have consequences. One consequence can be letting others down or letting yourself down. Can you live with that?
- Just be yourself.
- Trust your feelings. When your gut says no, choose a different action.
- Stand your ground.
- Say "No" and be assertive.
- Leave the scene and just walk away.
- Have a ready excuse such as "I have to go to the bathroom" or "My parents say that I have to go to a family event."
- Pretend that you didn't hear what was said and just walk away.
- Suggest a better idea.

Bullying

In all likelihood your child will experience bullying at school. She may not be the bully and she may never be bullied, but she will almost certainly see a bullying situation or hear about one. Your child may be on the giving end, bullying fellow students, on the receiving end, experiencing bullying from others, or she may be "sitting on the fence." It is ideal to arm your child with coping skills and defense mechanisms from a very early age. Bullying does not end once a child finishes school. It can happen well into adulthood and in the workplace, so good lifelong strategies are needed to help your child manage.

By definition, bullying at school is a situation in which one or more students single out another student and engage in negative actions with the intention of harm. It is an aggressive behavior and it is intentional. For the most part, bullying is repeated over time and there is an imbalance of power or strength between the students involved. The student being bullied may have trouble defending herself and feels afraid.

Bullying can take many forms, such as physical, verbal, emotional, relational bullying and cyber bullying. In direct bullying, the victim is confronted face to face. With indirect bullying, the victim is not confronted, but rumors are spread and she is laughed at behind her back. Being bullied is scary and hurtful to kids of all ages.

Types of Bullying

Physical bullying can involve hitting, punching, kicking, spitting, shoving, pushing, pinching and taking belongings.

Verbal bullying can involve teasing or name-calling, threats, laughing at, spreading rumors, mocking or insults.

Emotional bullying can involve intimidation, use of gestures, shunning, social exclusion or spreading nasty stories.

Relational bullying (mean girl syndrome): Relationships between girls can be very complicated. Most girls and women we have spoken to have, at one point or another in their lives, been the subject of rumors, lies or gossip, been betrayed, excluded or exposed to "the silent treatment" from other girls who were once good friends. This devastating type of bullying is not easy to detect as it is not always obvious. It is not physical, but it is verbal bullying and it happens in school hallways, washrooms, schoolyards, on the bus and online. How can parents help?

- Get your daughter involved in more than one social circle, for example, school friends, neighborhood friends, friends through a lesson or club. The broader a girl's social circle, the less chance there will be that she will be left feeling friendless if there is an incident at school.
- Talk about bullying in general, and relational bullying specifically, before it happens.
- Monitor your child's online activity.
- Report incidents of relational bullying to school authorities.

Cyber bullying involves sending insulting or threatening messages via text message, email, social networks or other communication technologies. It can include many forms such as name-calling, teasing, exclusion or threats. This type of bullying is usually much meaner because the bully never has to face the victim.

If a cyber bullying situation occurs, children should be told the following: don't respond, block the person, don't delete any messages and tell a parent what is happening.

The Bully

The bully is the child who is overbearing and aggressive, threatening other children in an intimidating way. Often, this child has no friends and the other children are afraid of her. Sometimes the bully is, in fact, popular and has the support of her peers.

Reasons vary as to why a child becomes a bully. It could be it a way to get attention, even though it is negative attention. Bullying behavior gives the child a feeling of power. It might be a distraction to cover up a sense of inadequacy. Maybe she has been a victim of bullying and is lashing out. She may never have learned how to deal with conflict in a peaceful way and has no coping skills. Bullying may be the one thing that she does well and with confidence to compensate for being weak in social and academic areas. The bully has little compassion or empathy toward others and may feel that she has the right to hurt others. A bully will usually continue if the victim doesn't complain and the witnesses remain quiet.

Internet Safety

Most schools have Internet safety programs for students to teach them how to be safe online. A few hints for Internet safety and computer use at home:

- Keep computers in an area where you can monitor your child.
- Be sure your child knows never to give out personal information on line or on social networks.
- Put parental controls on the computer.
- Limit the amount of time your child spends online. (This will vary by age.)
- Instruct your child never to add someone they do not know to a social network or instant messaging list.

The Bullied

The child being bullied is the victim who suffers from bullying and being picked on. It's not normal to be bullied and it isn't the child's fault. Some kids who are being bullied lack self-confidence and, consequently, they lack the strength needed to get help. The child blames herself and, in fact, somehow thinks that it is her fault. She may want to fit in so badly that she doesn't want to rock the boat or be seen as a "tattletale," so she allows the bullying to continue. It could also be that she is a peaceful, passive person who attracts the attention of the bully, who sees her as an "easy mark." A victim of bullying should never be told to ignore the situation, to retaliate or to sort it out all alone.

What to Do If Your Child Is Being Bullied

As a parent, you may notice a change in your child. Perhaps she seems anxious, is not eating or sleeping well, is moody and easily upset or doesn't want to go to school. These can be symptoms of many problems, so initiate a discussion and encourage your child to open up. If she confides in you that she is being bullied, offer comfort and support. Your child may feel ashamed and embarrassed. She may also feel that if the bully finds out that she has revealed what is going on, the situation will get worse for her.

Most schools have anti-bullying programs, policies and procedures aimed at making the school a safe place where every student feels secure. The school code of conduct contains expectations of good behavior and consequences for bullying. Teachers receive special training through workshops and at staff meetings. There are sometimes school counselors or specialized staff who provide information, assistance and guidance to teachers, parents and students. There are school-wide assemblies, presentations and initiatives designed to educate the students about peer pressure and bullying. A good classroom teacher provides strategies to help students deal with peer pressure and bullying situations through instruction, lessons, activities and role-playing.

If your child is being bullied at school, contact the teacher. Set up a meeting to discuss the problem. Share your concerns and ask for advice. The situation will be taken very seriously by school staff.

What to Tell a Child Who Is Being Bullied
- Don't blame yourself.
- Act confident and don't show fear.
- Stay away from the bully.
- Hang out with a group or with a buddy.
- Stay calm; don't react or engage in dialogue.
- Tell another student what is going on and enlist their help.
- Act as if you didn't hear and walk away.
- Tell the classroom or yard duty teacher.
- Tell your parents and ask for advice.
- If you are afraid to tell the teacher, confide in someone you trust.
- Arrange to speak with the principal or vice-principal.
- Write an anonymous note and drop it on the teacher's desk.

The Witnesses to Bullying

The kids who witness a bullying situation often do one of four things:
- Encourage the bully.
- Try to defuse the bullying situation and protect the victim.
- Stand by and do nothing. (They may be afraid of the bully themselves.)
- Report the bullying to a teacher or parent.

Ask your child if she has seen any bullying at school. Ask her how she and others dealt with it and brainstorm ideas and possible solutions for any future situations.

Children will most likely experience peer pressure and bullying at school in one form or another.

- Peer pressure can be positive, neutral or negative
- Talk with your child about strategies for dealing with negative peer pressure and bullying
- Work on character building with your child to help her deal with peer pressure and bullying
- Bullying can be physical, verbal or emotional
- Call the school immediately if your child is bullied

Chapter 14
Parenting Tips

Both of us were teachers before we had our own children. After we became moms, we found that a lot of the strategies we used in the classroom applied equally well at home. We didn't turn our homes into mini classrooms, but rather we took the common sense, organization and sense of humor that made our classrooms work and used it in raising our families.

Have we had tough days, rough patches and moments when we wanted to scream? Yes, both at home and at school. Everyone does. Have we also experienced success, been filled with happiness and felt a huge sense of accomplishment? Yes, both at home and at school. We are not experts, but we offer these tried and true, common sense ideas that you may find useful with your family.

Funny Book/Memory Box

When we started teaching together, we shared lots of stories about the funny things kids said and did. After a couple of years, we discovered that we had forgotten some of those hilarious things we thought we would remember forever. So we started "The Funny Book," a collection of sayings and stories from kids that you could never make up, even if you tried. It's a great idea to keep a notebook handy at home where you can scribble down your child's sayings, anecdotes and milestones.

We kept samples of student work on file or in a portfolio. You can do the same at home. You may be inundated with all the work brought home from school. One way of managing this is to have a container where all schoolwork is kept. Go through it periodically and have your child select a few pieces to keep. At the end of the school year, you and your child can choose a few pieces he is especially proud of or attached to, and transfer them to a file or a box that you will keep and add to from year to year.

Keep It Positive

In the classroom we tried to instill a positive attitude and keep the atmosphere upbeat. When speaking to and about students we tried to phrase things nicely, for example, "Please wait for your turn to speak" instead of "Don't interrupt." Children are more responsive when spoken to respectfully and we found that they began speaking to each other more kindly as well.

Empathy

It is very important for all of us, children and adults, to feel empathy for other people—to recognize, understand and identify with the feelings of those around us. In our classrooms, we work to build a strong sense of community and teamwork. Team building helps students see and show respect for the feelings and points of view of others.

Children develop empathy by seeing it modeled, especially by the significant adults in their lives, as well as through a lot of discussion. Talk with your child about possible explanations for the behavior of others, both real people as well as characters in books and movies. Ask your child, "How do you think that person feels?" Help your child understand body language and facial expressions, and the link between actions and feelings. Teach your child to try to understand both sides of a situation. Talk about your own feelings and encourage other family members to do so. Make acts of charity and kindness a family project. When your child displays empathetic behavior, point it out and praise him for it.

Studies have shown that people with a strong sense of empathy are able to form strong relationships and to work well as members of a team. What a great gift to give a child!

Routines

We discovered early on in our teaching careers the importance of routines. Students knew what to expect and when to expect it. Routines make a classroom run smoothly.

Routines also make a home run smoothly. Kids thrive on them. They will know what to do and when to do it. Establish routines early and adjust them as your child grows.

Calendar

We always had a large timetable and calendar displayed in the classroom. Children could look at it and prepare themselves by getting out the materials for the next subject and also know what they had to look forward to (or not) for the rest of the day. Even though you may keep an electronic calendar, post a wall calendar at home and update it regularly. It is a good organizer for the whole family and a place where school, extracurricular and social events can be marked down. If your child is young, look at the calendar together and plan what needs to go to school on any given day, for example, gym clothes. Older children can refer to the calendar independently. It gives them an opportunity to take responsibility, plan ahead and budget their time.

Humor

At school, humor helped us establish a good rapport with our students, keep things in perspective, cut the tension and brightened our days. We chose to see the cup as half full and not half empty and got our kids to do likewise. Seeing the humor in things does not mean making light of a serious situation, but it lightens the load and enables you to take a step back and look at things more objectively.

Keep It Simple

In the classroom we found that simple, concise explanations were the best explanations. Everybody understands clear and simple. To avoid questions like "I don't get it," explain things simply, make rules and consequences clear and uncomplicated, and "cut to the chase."

Be Organized

For a teacher, being organized is a life-saving strategy. It is also something teachers try to instill in their students. Being on top of deadlines, organizing your workspace and being prepared allows you to clear the clutter and get on with the task at hand. Time is not wasted. At home, being organized allows each family member to get where they need to be and do what they need to do quickly, efficiently and in a good frame of mind.

Read

Read, read, read.

Recess

Recess is built in to the school day and it is there for a reason. Kids need a break, they need to move around and they need fresh air.

This helps them clear their minds and they are able to refocus and get back to the work at hand after the break.

When working on chores, doing homework or sitting in front of the TV or computer, a break can be refreshing and reenergizing. And it's not just kids who benefit from breaks.

Trips

An out-of-classroom excursion, better known as the "class trip" is always a much-anticipated, out of the ordinary, memorable and much-talked about experience. Book learning pales in comparison. Children take knowledge from the classroom and apply it to what they experience on the trip or they learn something on the trip that they bring back to the classroom. And getting there is half the fun. The more experiences you provide for your child the better. Go for a walk in the woods, visit the zoo, seek out a local museum, find the nearest body of water, swim at your local community center. The list is endless.

Variety Is the Spice of Life

In the classroom, we tried to provide a variety of learning experiences for our students. Pencil and paper tasks, group work, watching a demonstration, listening to the teacher read, performing a skit and active learning are all part of every day life at school. At home, providing a mix of activities for your child will enrich her learning whether it is school or home related.

Follow Through

It is most important for kids to be able to believe, and to count on, the adults in their lives. At school if we said we were going to do something and did not follow through, we had dozens of unhappy kids pointing it out and holding us accountable. To keep our credibility intact, we had to make sure that it didn't happen very often. If we promised the class a reward or treat, the children looked forward to it and counted on us to be true to our word. Keeping promises builds a positive relationship between teacher and students. The same holds true when following through with consequences for misbehavior or broken rules. At school, children understand that there is an expected behavior. Children feel secure when they have boundaries and there is no doubt in their minds as to what will happen to them when they step outside those boundaries. When expectations are consistent and consequences are consistently applied, there is no confusion and everybody is happy.

Kids are used to boundaries and expectations at school. At home, boundaries and expectations are equally effective when followed through consistently. We often found that dealing with a classroom full of children at school was easier than handling our own children at home. It is worth the time and effort necessary to establish your "house rules" so that there is no confusion and everybody is happy.

Not Every Day Is a Good Day

Some days it all goes wrong. Pouring rain, indoor recess, fire drill, a kid throws up and you forgot your lunch on the kitchen counter. There's nothing you can do but wait for the day to be over. It happens at school, it happens at home, it happens at the office. Wipe the slate clean, have a good sleep, start fresh tomorrow.

Family Time

In the classroom, teacher and students spend a lot of time together as a "family" away from home. When the class is together there is back-and-forth talking, joking, listening, sharing and laughing. Each day when the class comes together, there is a lot of catch-up conversation about what happened last night or on the weekend.

Spend time together as a family. Make time every day to talk, laugh, discuss and share stories about the day. A great place for this is at the dinner table. Busy families can't always make this happen, but try to have a family meal together as often as you can. Take every opportunity to come together. Have fun with your kids. Every member of the family will benefit.

A Fine Balance

In the classroom many things are balanced—quiet time with noisy busy time, individual activities with group and whole class activities, a timetable is balanced between heavy subjects (Math) and lighter subjects (Art), and the class itself is balanced between boys and girls, students of varying abilities and personalities. It's good to have balance. At home, consider the balance between school work and extracurricular activities, family time and friend time, busy time and down time.

Savor the Moments

When we start teaching on the first day of school, the end of the year seems very far away. There are inevitably days in the middle of the year when the end can't come soon enough. Then, before you know it, it is the last day of school and we are sorry to see those kids walking out the door for the last time. The school year flies by in a flash.

Your kid's childhood will fly by in a flash. Don't miss it.

Many of the mindsets and organizational tools used in the classroom are helpful at home.

- Use common sense and humor, and have a positive attitude
- Make family time a priority and enjoy your child at every stage of growing up
- Establish routines, boundaries and consequences and be sure to follow through
- Stay organized by using calendars, memory boxes and a notebook

Recommended Reading

Alexander-Roberts, Colleen. *The ADHD Parenting Handbook: Practical Advice for Parents from Parents*. Dallas, Tex.: Taylor Pub., 1994.

American Girl, ed. *What I Wish You Knew: Letters From Our Daughters' Lives, and Expert Advice on Staying Connected*. Middleton, WI: Pleasant, 2001.

Braun, Betsy Brown. *Just Tell Me What to Say: Sensible Tips and Scripts for Perplexed Parents*. New York: Collins, 2008.

Campito, Jan Starr. *Supportive Parenting: Becoming an Advocate for Your Child with Special Needs*. London: Jessica Kingsley, 2007.

Coloroso, Barbara. *Kids Are Worth It!: Raising Resilient, Responsible, Compassionate Kids*. Toronto: Penguin Canada, 2010.

Coloroso, Barbara. *The Bully, the Bullied, and the Bystander: From Preschool to High School—How Parents and Teachers Can Help Break the Cycle of Violence*. New York: HarperResource, 2004.

Faber, Adele, Elaine Mazlish, and Kimberly Ann. Coe. *How to Talk So Kids Will Listen & Listen So Kids Will Talk*. New York: Collins Living, 2004.

Fertig, Carol. *Raising a Gifted Child: A Parenting Success Handbook*. Waco, Tex.: Prufrock Press, 2009.

Pueschel, Siegfried M. *A Parent's Guide to Down Syndrome: Toward a Brighter Future*. Baltimore, MD: Paul H. Brookes Pub., 2008.

Scieszka, Jon. *Guys Write for Guys Read*. New York: Viking, 2005.

Simmons, Rachel. *Odd Girl Out: The Hidden Culture of Aggression in Girls*. New York: Harcourt, 2002.

Smith, Corinne Roth., and Lisa W. Strick. *Learning Disabilities A to Z: A Parent's Complete Guide to Learning Disabilities from Preschool to Adulthood*. New York: Free Press, 1997.

Wiseman, Rosalind. *Queen Bees and Wannabes: Helping Your Daughter Survive Cliques, Gossip, Boyfriends, and Other Realities of Her Life*. New York: Three Rivers Press, 2009.

Web Resources

Dictionary.com: www.dictionary.com

EasyBib: www.easybib.com

Encyclopedia: www.encyclopedia.com

Google: www.google.com

Guys Read: www.guysread.com

Quotations at Bartleby.com: www.bartleby.com/quotations

teAchnology: www.teach-nology.com

Thesaurus.com: www.thesaurus.com

Wikipedia: www.wikipedia.com

Acknowledgments

Betty and Laura would like to thank:

Kathy Fraser, our very hands-on editor, thanks for navigating us through the process with expertise and good humor;

Scot Ritchie, a great illustrator and such a good sport;

The people at Firefly Books;

Joseph Gisini and Andrew Smith at PageWave Graphics for a great book design;

Carol Bonnett, for finishing touches

Betty would like to thank:

My family, Steve, Katie, Tess and James, Morgan, Julia and Amelia, all my love;

Laura Mayne, thanks for the adventure of a lifetime!;

My brother Rick Borowski, our math guru;

My sister Helen Borowski and my friend Kathy Parker for listening

Laura would like to thank:

My family, Moo, Mary and Brian, Tom, Rob and Liza, Jenn, Matt and Erin;

Betty. So much fun, so much laughter. We did it!;

Betty's family, Steve, Tessa and James, Kate, Morgan, Julia and Amelia for their support and friendship;

James Parkinson, thank you once again from Anne F. Bancroft;

John, for words on rocks;

Patrick O'Kelly, who cheerfully pointed out that this book is proof that I am not a "one hit wonder"

Contributors

*Special thanks
to all those who
contributed:*
Stephen Abram,
  our library and
  research expert
Gay Baile for special
  education advice
Rick Borowski (of
  CanAm.*Pi*) for
  math guidance
Mary Ann Burrows
  for the funniest
  and most touching
  contribution
Marina Nemat for
  her encouragement
Kristin Hohenadel
  for author photos
Siena Perrotta for
  sharing her story
Dagmar Batz
James Biss
Dallas Borris
Sonia Boston
Nancy Bourque
Barb Butler
Elspeth Cameron
John Campbell
Joan Cobbold
Deb Conderan
Siobhan Connor-
  Philips
Carol Dineen

Kim Donaldson
Robyn Dony
Kate Dyer
Stephen Dyer
Gord Farley
Marilyn Ferley
Rita Feutl
Alice Ficko
Marilyn Filice
Dawn Foster
Moira Franke
Laura Fraser
Mary Fraser
Janice Gomes
Erin Gumieniak
Rob Gumieniak
Joel Hanna
Heather Hase
Valerie Hatton
Chris House
Luke Hohenadel
Paola Hohenadel
Mindy Inglese
Christine Kluczynski
Lara Ladwig
Rhona Lahey
Tina Lamb
Angela Langlois
Charlotte Leavitt
Kirk Lemon
Stefani Linse
Patrick Maguire
Dianna Malho
Gerard Mayne

Maddy Mayne
Robyn McCullough
Moe McLauchlin (of
  Educational Help
  Centres, Inc.)
Lisa Neamtz
Gloria O'Brien
Jen O'Hannesin
Dayna O'Kelly
James Parkinson
Ed Pernu
Donna Perry
Gabriele Pizzale
Joe Pizzale
Derek Saliba
Jo-Ann Saliba
Wendy Shirey
Jackie Smalls
Stephanie Smith-
  Abram
Tom Sraver
Marc St. Martin
Lis Valeriote
Sandra Valeriote
Adri Van Hilten
Tessa Vandenhoek
Angela Veinot
Carol Weber
Fatima Wittemund

and all the students
and parents we
had the pleasure of
knowing

Index